bliss now

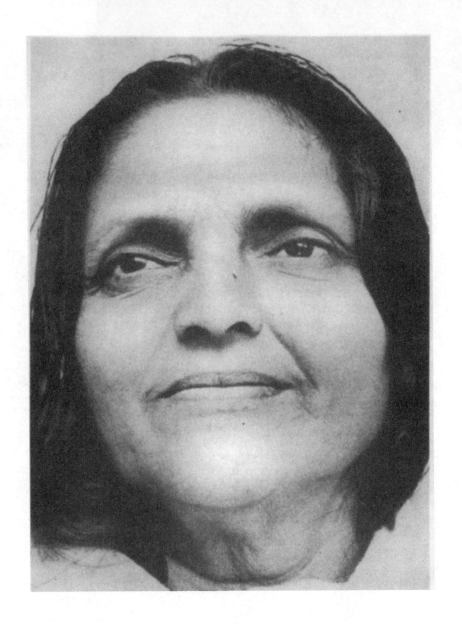

Sri Sri Anandamayi MA

Bliss Now

My journey with
Sri Sri Anandamayi Ma

by
Swami Ramananda

select books
optimizing the publishing process

Published by SelectBooks, Inc.
For information contact SelectBooks, Inc., New York, New York.

Cover and text design and production by Mayapriya, Bookwrights Design, www.bookwrights.com

Cover photo by Yogiraj: "Swamiji, the happiest man I know."

Edited lovingly by Prema Das (Ruth M. Nolan, M.A.)
Photos (in addition to those credited in the text) by Ananda, Krishna Priya, Prema Das, Saraswati, Sudama, Tara Devi, and by/courtesy of Swami Ramananda. All photos of Anandamayi Ma, unless otherwise noted, courtesy of Swami Ramananda

Printed in the United States of America
ISBN 1-59079-019-7
Library of Congress Control Number 2002092884

Library of Congress Cataloging in Publication Data
Swami Ramananda
    Bliss Now

This book is dedicated with love to the undying spirit of Sri Sri Ek Sri Anandamayi Ma and placed with mahabhava on her Lotus Feet.

This book is lovingly dedicated to my mother.

If a lowly rogue like me can become a swami,
there is hope for everyone.

भारत
INDIA

1 00

श्री श्री माँ आनन्दमयी
SHREE SHREE MA ANANDAMAYEE
1987

"By doing japa and meditation of Krishna, by loving Him, His attraction should become so powerful that even suffering is cherished. Therefore, meditating on Him alone, dedicating all actions to Him, be an instrument in His hands. Keeping your body—His temple—clean and pure, immersed in the thought of Him, endeavor to let all our actions be permeated by Krishna. He is all that is experienced. The man who can be engrossed in Him, in joy and sorrow, in every one of his actions, in the midst of worldly life that is ruled by the mind—that man will be victorious."

—Sri Sri Anandamayi MA, from *Matri Vani*, Vol II, verse 232

CONTENTS

blessing

In this book, Swami Ramananda demonstrates the beauty of devotion through his words, faith, and positive attitude. His joyfulness and complete surrender to God/Goddess is a perfect example of 'living love.' Swamiji's exuberant bhakti pours forth the blessing of the great renowned mystic, the Holy Mother Anandamayi Ma. Allow Her grace to flow through his words, and open your heart to pure love. Meet Swami Ramananda in his inspiring story, and journey into *Bliss Now*.

—Baba Bhagavan Das

photo by Saraswati

foreword

I have known Swami Ramananda since he was seventeen years old. At the time I found him, he was wandering in the Himalayas like a young sadhu. I saw in him, tremendous spiritual potential, and the reincarnation of a very old, significant soul. He became my protege, and together, we wandered the spiritual ashrams of India for nearly seven years.

Very bright, a quick learner, and astute with language skills, Swamiji became a great adept of the yoga I taught in the Sivananda lineage. We visited intimately and privately with some of the greatest saints of India living at that time. We took the darshan of my dear friend, the Maharishi Mahesh Yogi, who initiated Ramananda personally and privately in Transcendental Meditation, in his meditation chamber in Rishikesh. We spent a great deal of time with Sri Tat Wala Baba, and Ramananda stayed with him in his cave for a period of time. We traveled high, near the source of the Ganges to Gangotri, where Ramananda was introduced to many saints and naga babas, most who are no longer with us today. Intimate insights on yoga were shared with him, and he was privy to certain papers, describing spiritual states leading to siddhis, that probably no other eye has seen.

At all times, Ramananda has been my dear student and companion pilgrim. For many months, we stayed in the Hall of Swamis, built over the Ganges at Sivananda Ghat. It was from this vantage point that he met his Guru, Sri Sri Anandamayi MA, and came deeply under the influence of MA's lila. MA appointed me as his personal teacher, and we have continued this relationship now for thirty-three years.

MA instructed me that at a certain time in Ramananda's sadhana, he was to take full initiation as a Swami, and that he was to accept those duties and responsibilities. I was happy to perform this initiation on Ramananda in the Ganges during the Khumba Mela we attended together in Allahabad. At the time, I named Swami Ramananda Shiva Das, my dharma successor, as well. We have had many years of holy yogic sadhana together.

❖

Of all the persons I know of who were intimately around Sri Sri Anandamayi MA, perhaps Swami Bashkaranandaji and Ramananda most appear to carry Mother's shakti. I have never seen either one of them in a moment when they were not living in a deep and lasting bliss.

Witnessing Ramananda and Mother in the same room was a powerful and moving experience. There seemed to be a powerful electricity between the two of them. From the way Mother looked at Ramananda, there was no question that he was Her son completely. From his very first darshan of Sri Anandamayi MA, I noticed a considerable change in his appearance. He instantly became a new person, floating in a deep bhava. I watched him move into many trance states in Her presence, and he walked away pure and glowing, as if he were the moon, reflecting Her dazzle.

Now, seeing Swami Ramananda at this age, so deeply seated in bliss and peace, I feel my work is done. We have made seventeen pilgrimages across India, from Tamil Nadu to the Himalayas, and have visited most major ashrams and great living teachers there. I often reflect on the glorious experiences and the laughter we have shared, and although we have spent years of quiet times together, often being together without speaking for weeks, I feel that I have come to know Swamiji inside and out. He is authentically who he says he is. He is at all moments sincere. He is in a deep state of bliss and samadhi. He appears to be in direct communication with Sri Anandamayi MA. He says he sees Her with him at all times. There is a glow in his countenance, and everyone who meets him feels an electric presence.

I highly recommend this book to you. You are a blessed soul to find your way to him. Take your time with this book. Make a quiet cup of tea, and let your heart soar in this journey we will share with you. This is not just a physical journey, but the story of Swamiji finding his Guru. It is a journey that will take you within your own soul.

May each and every one of you find a lasting friendship in your own heart with Sri Anandamayi MA. She was the greatest teacher I have ever witnessed in India. With my own eyes, I never once saw Her waver from Her pure course of work in this world. She was constantly blissful, and Her joy was infectious. She has left us with such a bright son in Ramananda, who only cares to share Her light. She said to us, "Take this light to all the children who cannot come here to be with their Mother." May this book make your heart sing.

Om Namah Shivaya! Jai MA!

Swami Shankarananda Shiva Das Giri
Acharya of the Adi Parashakti Shiva
Peetha, Rishikesh.

prologue

If there is one great quality all spiritual persons possess in common, it is the quality of BLISS. In spite of the challenging times we live in, I would like to give everyone permission to be HAPPY, and to search inwardly for lasting Bliss. Sometimes, I think that if I see one more sullen, unhappy yoga teacher, I will say, "you should take us to bliss!" The greatest yogis and gurus I have been intimately with (Sri Sri Anandamayi MA, Sri Neem Karoli Baba, Maharishi Mahesh Yogi, Swami Satchidananda, Tat Wala Baba, Sri Swami Shankarananda Giri, and so many, many more) were in ecstatic states of bliss. The laughter never stops around them. . .even when there is death, destruction, war, avarice, crime, they are laughing at life, at the human condition, at MAYA. It is our sense of humor, our laughter, and our lightheartedness as human beings that make us truly great. May I please, as a Swami, say to all you yogis out there: "LIGHTEN UP!"

My Guru, Sri Sri Anandamayi MA, would fall into such fits of laughter that we had to fan Her and give Her water so that She could catch Her breath. Mother's laughter was infectious, and She had the power to make even the most sullen intellectual pundits smile. She even made Indira Gandh i smile! Life is just not that foreboding; only if you believe that life is a horrible reality, and only if you get caught up in all of this MAYA, can you walk through life being so unhappy! MA would not have it! She would find a way to crack that smile with a hit or a pinch if She had to!

Where I live in India, there are homeless people living in metal lean-tos against the wall of my compound. I know one woman who is raising fourteen children by herself, without even a roof over her head. She cleans her children daily, and lines them up and feeds them, cooking their food right on the street, and yet every day, when I walk from my gate, she greets me with the most gorgeous smile I have ever seen. Her children have beautiful teeth, because they cannot afford candy, and they all call out to me in Tamil, "Varnakum, Swamiji!" These are fifteen of the most beautiful, genuine smiles I have ever seen; they are smiles that refuse to lose hope, even in

photo courtesy of Swami Ramananda

the face of tremendous poverty; they are smiles that emanate from the rich knowledge that God lives within, and is accessible equally to everyone, regardless of wealth, material possessions, or caste. To me, this is the real wealth of INDIA: its unshakeable faith! This wealth is the knowledge that God is within every human heart, no matter how clouded by evil, how lost, how neglected, or how hidden. God is sitting there within each of us, waiting for discovery! Those impoverished children in India are wealthier than many of the millionaires I know in Beverly Hills.

❖

When I come home to Los Angeles and walk down the streets of Rodeo Drive, I am confronted with such spiritual poverty that I become ill! No one smiles, and everyone is rushing, pushing, and hurrying off. . .to what!? Everyone seems to be trying to get more toys, trying to get ahead, and spending money with credit they don't have. They are miserable. . .miserable. . .miserable. I think back to those children in India, in their poverty, with their sweet, humble smiles. They will do anything for a few pennies, just so they might put a little rice and a few simple vegetables on their table, if they are lucky. Like the lark, they will sing all day long for just a few berries. In their resplendent bhava, their joyous poverty, they put us to shame.

We in the West should be the most joyous of people. We should be the most grateful for our food markets, which are stacked with the best produce, the most delicious delicacies, and the most sophisticated products anywhere. Most Americans live like Maharajas, in our beautiful palaces with our wonderful cars. Even the poorest of our poor would be considered blessed in India. Where is the gratitude, and where is the joy, at such grace from God? Where is the peace that comes from the security of having so much abundance?

It's time for us all to take a reassessment of ourselves. Look at yourself, and make a list of everything you are thankful for. Look at all of the wonderful creature comforts that surround you. Feel some joy for your life, and for everything that is good: for your money, for your job, for your car, for your lovely family. . .and stop taking so much for granted!

LAUGH, LOVE, AND LIFT. Embrace a tree, smell a rose, give a stranger a hug. . .LET'S START living again. Too many people in America come to my yoga classes WAY TOO STRESSED OUT. I am seeing kids in their twenties with nervous conditions. Where is our spirituality? Where is the time to meditate? Where is the peace? It all seems so evasive, and yet it is all here at your fingertips.

You can live a godly life of total happiness. If you are lost, come to me. . .I will show you the way. I am a Swami, and that is what I am here for. I am here helping, guiding students, teaching yoga, and singing God's praises. Giving out hugs and smiles and love and laughter is all that this body is made for! Pull yourself out into the LIGHT. Now is the time to start living the life you were born to live. Now is the time to start accomplishing what you came here to Earth to accomplish. Time is fleeting away. . .we are all on death's doorstep in this violent, volatile world, with nuclear bombs pointed at everyone, and biological and chemical warfare on the rise. . .who knows if we will even be here tomorrow? The time is NOW! Now is the time to go within and start loving everything God is doing for you in this very moment.

May I give you permission to feel BLISS? May I give you permission to LAUGH at life's seeming ups and downs, and to even laugh at your own death, which is an illusion? May I give you permission to PLAY, and to enjoy this precious life? May I give you permission to SMILE, to DANCE, and to be the special snowflake that you truly are?!

This book is the YOGA of LAUGHTER. It is the yoga I have been sent into the world to bring to you. It is the teaching and the life of Sri Sri Anandamayi MA, the joy-permeated Mother of India, the master of all smiles, who, in Her delightful perfection pulled the heartstrings of every soul She met. When I close my eyes, I hear Her laughter. I see Her lovely, joyful face looking at my soul, and I know we are all blessed to enjoy the BLISS of this moment, even if we do nothing else with these lives. Feel the Bliss. . .oh my child, practice the YOGA OF LAUGHTER, Ananda Lila.

—Swami Ramananda
Jai Ma Ashram
Rancho Mirage, CA
April 15, 2002

photo by Sudama

❖

my journey with anandamayi ma

by Julian Yatra

Lord Shiva and Parvati with Ganesha

❈

the awakening

There are single moments of life that seem so beyond time. In those moments, we are eternal and bright beings on a small planet that is lost in space. The play of life on earth seems to defy all logic and reason…and yet, with each year of life, I am convinced that there are no coincidences. There does seem to be a golden master plan, and somehow, we are taught, even by our dreams. What great forces are at play here which give touch to our every desire? And what sort of grace reaches down to make sure that we meet all our teachers, in just the right time and place? There is something very exquisite underlying this creation, something so soft and subtle, yet in its utter simplicity, we are being taught and watched each and every moment, somewhere in time's illusory hour.

I always awaken at 2:15 a.m. It is the moment at which I was born. I am ten years old, and I have just had an incredible dream. I lie awake, looking at the ceiling, remembering that this is the same dream I had the week before, and the week before that. It is always the same dream, night after night, like some ancient programming.

"I am your Mother. Come to India!" the woman with the long, dark hair and beautiful, angelic face is always calling to me. Who is she? Why India? These are perplexing questions for a ten-year-old child. I lie awake, pondering the ceiling, and finally decide to tell my mother about these recurring dreams. The dream is so simple, and yet so haunting.

My mother was a beautiful woman with raven black hair, and brown eyes that danced like the Nile. She always had a smile and a soothing touch, and her words flowed like poetry. I knew she would know. She knew everything.

"Mother, I am having this dream night after night about a beautiful lady who is telling me she is my mother, and that she wants me to come to India. What does it mean?"

My mother looked at me pensively, shocked, and yet not shocked to hear such things come from my mouth. She was accustomed to hearing her unusual boy say the most mysterious things. I was a boy who had mastered Chopin and who was reading *The Iliad* and *The Odyssey* at the age of ten, and who was obsessed with reading *The Ramayana* over and over again. "You must always pay attention to your dreams, my son," she wisely said. "This woman is your Guide. Try to remember everything she says to you…"

Ah, the luck and good fortune of having an enlightened mother! How those words would ring in my heart for the rest of my journey!

🌰 🌰 🌰

I lived in the pulsing heart of the unrest of the mid-1960's at the University of California, Berkeley, dodging tear gas canisters and listening to the cries of anti-war marches. I crossed the waterfall on Strawberry Creek, and made my way to Hindi class. I was determined to request an audience with Dr. Haridas Chaudhuri. I knew that he knew.

"Dr. Chaudhuri, I have had a recurring dream throughout my life. I feel that you can somehow help me with it."

A genuinely spiritual man, he looked at me with complete compassion as I spoke.

"A beautiful woman with long, black hair is calling to me. She tells me she is my mother, and she always says, 'Come to India!'"

Dr. Chaudhuri's eyes mist with tears. He comes closer, hanging on to my shoulders, and looks directly into my soul.

"Then you must go. I can arrange it for you through the Mother of the Sri Aurobindo Ashram. You go to India, and you search for your mother. When such a dream occurs, you must answer the call. You can study from there, and I will give you credit here."

The next thing I knew, I was on a plane to India. It was a big thing to go to India in the 1960's; it was like space travel to another planet. Can you imagine a country more unlike the West than India? In the 1960's, a trip to India was like going back two hundred years in time. Most villages had no electricity. There were very few cars; only cabinet ministers and wealthy movie stars had them.

In the India of the 1960's, there was a war waging with Pakistan, and very often, food and living supplies were scarce. China had just turned the Dalai Lama and the Tibetans out of Tibet. People would come stumbling out of the Himalayas, starving and wearing only the rags on their backs. Women pulled plows in fields. There was no television. If you owned a bicycle, you were considered a truly wealthy person. People would line up nightly at my garbage can twenty people deep, to eat my leftovers. This was the India of the 1960's…still very ancient, very dusty, very traditional…and untouched by the modern world.

The British had been kicked out of India in 1948, and in the twenty years since then, the Indian people were finally free to be Hindu once again. After four hundred years of English influence, there was a great magical resurgence of faith. With this wave, some very special snow-flakes were appearing in a pantheon of modern gurus, who were edged out of the closet by Paramahansa Yogananda's exposure in the book, *Autobiography of a Yogi*. Beautiful ashrams were starting to sprout all over India, thanks to the patronage of wealthy Indians and eccentric Americans who somehow found their way to spiritual India.

In the 1960's, one could literally walk from ashram to ashram across the subcontinent, and be housed, fed, and filled with spirit. With American money, you could live like a king, as the rupee was so severely devalued. This made it possible to travel anywhere in India by train, stay at wonderful ashrams, and study with gurus, even on the most meager student income. This truly fit the hippie lifestyle, and beckoned hundreds of young seekers from the West to the mystical Indian shores.

I left my plane in New Delhi, and entered city streets filled with camels, oxen pulling carts, and gypsies dancing with tiny monkeys. Not even five paces out of the airport, a man sat playing with a cobra! India was like another planet. It was hard to believe that America and India could even exist on the same planet! I loved walking in the incredible atmosphere of the bazaars, where Indian women shopped and walked around barefoot, wearing nose rings and resplendent silk saris.

You step off the plane and you are in a world of ancient temples, scurrying monkeys, and priests, who chant and carry statues of multi-armed goddesses through the streets. You instantly feel as if you are in a trance…the drone of the tamboura invades your mind. You are assaulted in every direction by thousands of people, all of them very individualistic, each with their own color, their own style, and their own religion; each is also very, very ethnic; India has this kind of diversity. Everything is handmade, and there are thousands of craftspeople everywhere…carving, painting, sculpting, sewing, beading, and rolling incense. You feel surrounded in organic creativity. I love that. India is a whole country of funky, hand-crafted things. People wear the most beautiful clothing and diamond nose rings…it's a whole country of barefooted people!

This INDIA of the 1960's was my kind of place…it had to have been the coolest place on Earth. It was a dream!

Dr. Chaudhuri had arranged for me to return home to Pondicherry. After a brief visit to Old Delhi, I was flying over South India, with its vast forests of windswept coconut palms and ancient granite temples soaring to the skies…

photo courtesy of Swami Ramananda

pondicherry dreams

I headed to my former early childhood home in Pondicherry, South India. Pondicherry is the perfect blend of East and West. It is the French idea of what India should look like, and like all French colonies, it is filled with beautiful, decaying French architecture that is blended with Indian style and grace. Delightful white sand beaches are lined by stunning formal French gardens, which are full of neatly trimmed hedges, and colorful tropical flowers. The gardens are flanked by banyan trees, which are filled with cages of white cockatoos.

I loved to stroll along the promenade along the beach, where there are statues of Mahatma Gandhi, Joan of Arc, and Governor Joseph Francis Dupleix, who ruled Pondicherry as the French Governor in the 18th century. The stately Raj Nivas, a white marble colonial mansion in the center of the square, is a testimony to the French patronage of "Pondy," as it is affectionately called in the Tamil Nadu language.

In the Vieux Carre, or old French section of Pondicherry, next to the sea, is the marvelous Ashram of Sri Aurobindo and The Mother. My former home was located among these old, white French buildings, which have the look and atmosphere of the old French sections of New Orleans and the Casbah. There are such beautiful courtyards, fountains, and incredible gardens. This is the perfect atmosphere for meditation and contemplation, where, in the words of The Mother, "la Sagesse, ce que l'oeil de la vision divine voit en l'espirit!"

Sri Aurobindo was a great Indian freedom fighter, and formerly a professor at Baroda University. Because of his dynamic vision for India's freedom from England, he was pursued across India all the way to Pondicherry, where he sought refuge from prison with the French government, which never cared for England's interests in India. There, he teamed up with Mira Alphasa, a marvelous, psychic Parisian socialite, to form his ashram, which he based upon the higher minded truths of life lead to the earthly realization of the life divine, and to the evolution of the supermind (the high nirvana achieved by his yoga, and evolution to a transformed mind.)

Mira became "The Mother" to all of South India, and her powers were thought by all to be remarkable. She and Sri Aurobindo would give powerful darshans, during which they both would be seated on thrones covered with tiger skins. She would wear glorious, hand-painted silk saris, along with a gold and diamond tiara, which made her look like an ancient Indian cinema queen. The presence of these two powerful spiritual personalities was not to be taken lightly. There was such energy around both of them that many people were literally frozen, and could not move when they received their darshan.

Sri Aurobindo spent his days and nights in literary tapasya. He wrote extensive volumes on philosophy and poetry. He wrote the longest poem in the English language, "Savitri," which contains over fifty thousand stanzas. Because of his extensive education at Cambridge University in London, where he earned top honors, he was able to clearly articulate the pathways to enlightenment in Jnana Yoga, or mental yoga, from an intellectual point of view.

The Mother was constantly working in the world, building schools, hospitals, gyms and swimming pools. She would do anything for the advancement of Sri Aurobindo's ideals. Her presence was everywhere in Pondicherry. When I first arrived, she said to me, "I will be your sponsor in India; waste not your time. Furthermore, I have taken you deep within my consciousness. Your life will be very blessed. Study deeply and inwardly, and let not one stone go unturned. Live every moment of every day in prayer, and be happy at all times."

When promoting the ideas and philosophies of Sri Aurobindo, The Mother was the most unusual combination of Asian Queen and brute, formidable force. She attended to every detail in the ashram, and her loving touch was everywhere, in building designs, gardens, occult schools, incense factories, handmade paper, cottage industries, and a huge publishing house for Guruji's works.

The whole place exuded a high-minded idealism of utopia, and was full of French bohemian Parisians dressed in flowing white silk as they sipped chai in cafes like the "Tous Qu'il Faut," or the "All You Need," which was owned by The Mother's granddaughter. Peacocks, blue hyacinth macaws, and monkeys scampered in nearby banyan trees. The Mother often headed out for a weekend on a private island of artists, sailing in a boat that was shaped like a peacock and carved of pure Sandalwood. It was a dream of India that came from storybooks, and The Mother did everything within her powers, which were extensive, to make it real.

I would sit with her, staring into her deep green eyes, and listen to her read in French about the transformation of every human cell. What a spiritual powerhouse she was! As if that wasn't enough, I could always sit near the mahasamadhi of Sri Aurobindo! The enormous marble tomb felt more like a launching pad. If I placed my head over the saint's grave, I could see and feel it visibly shaking. Rather than experiencing peace, I felt as if I had been filled with rocket fuel!

Pondicherry was just this magical. I thanked Dr. Chaudhuri every day for sending me there, for I could not imagine any place in the world where one could study yoga so completely…and yet still, I was haunted by my dream.

One warm day in August, I drew up the courage to approach The Mother and ask her if the dream was about her. She was very old then. I approached her in her room for a private audience. She sat there, bathed in a green-golden light, like an alien queen from another world. She turned her head turned toward me, a stern look on her face.

"Your answer lies for you in the Himalayas," she said. Then, she handed me a plumaria flower, and whispered into my ear…"TRANSFORMATION." I left The Mother, and tried to ride my bicycle back to Auroville, but the power of her shakti had overwhelmed me. I had to lay the bike down twice by the side of the road to digest the experience. Then, I immediately began making plans to start a pilgrimage across India to the Himalayas.

Auroville Ashram was such an amazing place. It was the Mother's idea of the future. There was a huge temple in the shape of a giant sphere in the center of the city. It was completely covered with huge brass orbs that would move in the wind like a giant wind chime. Here, The Mother had placed a bit of soil from every country in the world, and sealed it in a large lotus urn. Extremely modern architecture was everywhere, set against the ancient Tamil landscape. People there lived so Zen-like, in a stark environment that smacked of Parisian ethnic minimalism. Beautiful, blonde children with blue eyes spoke Tamil to me. "The Sun-eyed children of a golden dawn," Sri Aurobindo says, in, "Savitri".

With just my small backpack, which contained just one dhoti and my dhunda, I headed to the huge Ganesha temple in downtown Pondy. This has to be one of the most beautiful Ganesha temples in all of India. The story is that a former Catholic French governor ordered that the temple idol of Ganapati be sunk in the bay, near Ceylon. He was convinced that this would stop the idol worship in his province. The next day, however, the Ganesha re-appeared back in the sanctum sanctorium of the temple. He ordered its sinking three times. Each time, the idol came back to the temple. This miracle so overwhelmed the governor that he converted to Hinduism, and his family has been devoted to Ganesha ever since. I took a powerful darshan of Ganesha, and asked him to remove the obstacles in my spiritual path, so that I could find my Mother.

I headed for the busy bus station, and boarded a bus to Adayar, which is located near Madras. The bus headed out along the old beach road, and traveled the ocean through beautiful, small villages, such as Mahabalipuram, where I arrived at sunset. The sky was crimson around the old shore temple, which was built right on the beach some two thousand years ago. There, the waves dash against a lingam, and shoot high in the air. It is said that once there were seven temples there, but that the sea has claimed them all, except for this final, beautiful granite temple built in the Cholla style. One great temple there is made of huge, carved snakes, and is a temple to the naga babas. When descending the ancient stone stairs to the basement shrine, one is greeted by hundreds of slithering cobras.

As the bus next crosses the sleepy countryside, I can see the great gopurams that are so characteristic of the Dravidian style rising high into the air, like ancient skyscrapers of the tropical landscape. The sides are carved with erotic sculptures of the loves and dalliances of the gods, and look as if they have simply emerged from the earth and been there since the beginning of time.

❊

Blavatsky's Loka

When we arrived in Adayar, it was dawn, and the first rays of Surya were shimmering across the beautiful Adayar River. Huge water buffalo floated among the lotus blossoms on the water's edge, and waded all the way to the ocean at the mouth of the river. Fishermen, silhouetted against the red rays of dawn, threw their morning nets and appeared to be walking on the water in the shallows. In my heart and mind, there could be no place on earth more magical than this India.

In Adayar, I stayed at the Theosophical Society compound. It was a walled banana and coconut plantation of nearly one thousand acres, developed by Madame Blavatsky as her home in India. She had collected gorgeous species of flora and fauna from all over the world. I was assigned quarters in a huge colonial mansion, "Blavatsky Bungalow," where daily I saw the box where letters addressed to her arrived from the Tibetan masters. In the front yard was the largest banyan tree in the world, spanning nearly 44,000 square feet; it was completely filled with white cockatoos. I would stroll daily to the beautiful "Hindoo Temple" she had built in white granite, with the different dancing poses from Bharata Natyam carved into the columns. There, I would gather my daily water in a brass pot and walk amongst the cannonball trees, which would burst into clusters of red flowers when a person passed by them in the jungle.

My days and nights at the Theosophical Society were resplendent. There, I was walled away from the world, and lived in a psychic's idea of what India should be: filled with temples representing all of the world's major religions; rich with windswept coconuts trees, where tiny beige monkeys played; and ripe with a view of the Adayar River, which was filled with crocodile-covered islands and a private white sand beach, which was accessible only by making one's way through a dense, tropical jungle. One day, I sat in the jungle and watched nearly one hundred baboons devour the tangerine trees as they swept through on vines like Tarzan; they looked so much like a living Rousseau painting. Oftentimes, in my treks to the beach, I would encounter

Blavatsky's personal Kyodo dragon, which was nearly seven feet long. Needless to say, as I knew I was on the dragon's food chain, I would seek shelter in a tree and let her pass!

What a spectacular, magical place was this sacred place in the 1960's. . .filled with the most eccentric British ladies, who would have teas on their roof gardens wearing lavender frocks and huge floral hats, their servants in tailored red turbans serving pound cake, as peacocks strutted about on the rooftop. One lady told me she had her servants move her bed to the jungle — quite a huge English bed of carved mahogany and yards of draped mosquito netting — for "more psychic intensity!"

Another lady in a large, green polka dot hat told me that if I squinted my eyes just so, I could see that all the fairies on the property had golden wings tinged with azure. It was at these ladies' insistence that the huge lock was broken on Madame Blavatsaky's private chamber, and that I was the first person in one hundred years allowed to enter, so that I could play the pipe organ she had brought all the way from England. I brushed away the cobwebs, and touched the stained ivory keys, which had only been touched by the great Blavatsky. As I started playing a Bach fugue, dust blew out of the pipes like a giant steam engine. The sound of the organ was dark and dismal against the tropical, star-dotted sky. "Divine!" exclaimed Miss Priscilla Beetram, and all the ladies clapped loudly at the end of my concert. Then, the room was ceremoniously closed and locked in silence, as if to preserve even the dust left by the great Blavatsky.

I had quite lost touch with any sense of time at the Theosophical compound, and I spent my days in idyllic splendor, hiking in the coconut palms, placing flowers at the Hindu temples, and meditating by the river's edge, where I looked across at the vast palace of the Maharaja of Chennai. One day, while meditating as the water buffalo waded through the lotus flowers at the river's edge, I saw a stirring in the fallen leaves near my feet. Suddenly, a king cobra raised itself with hood fully extended, and stared right into my face. I pulled myself from my meditation, pranamed to the cobra, and said, "Brother!" The cobra stared at me, as if shocked at my stillness and lack of reaction. It turned and looked out at the river, and then started to move away down the river's edge. It would only go a few feet, and stop and look back at me. In all my life, I had never witnessed such nobility in an animal. I felt exceedingly blessed by this encounter.

 # crossing india

I boarded the Madras Mail for New Delhi amidst a whirlwind of beggars, weary travelers, and a barrage of rikshaws. The rikshaw boy grabbed my luggage, and boarded the train a hundred feet ahead of me. As I made my way through the crowds, I thought I would never see my luggage again.

When the conductor helped me find my way to my first class suite, there were my luggage and dhoti, hanging in the armoire. What an exquisite way to travel! I watched India pass by as I sat at the small desk at the window. As I sat writing in my journal, my attendant, who was wrapped in a smart red turban, would appear and offer me chai and samosas. Words were flowing like a river of poetry.

❈

"Against the steady click clack of the train on the track, great giant temples appear, even in the smallest towns and most insignificant countryside. Rising gopurams are covered with the dances of the gods. Great stone gateways echo to some ancient melody past. Silvan swamps are lined with coconut palms, where monkeys scamper about an island temple, and a lone sitarist plays, wearing a bright sari of fuscia and emerald green…"

I was in a trance state, so in love with the India passing my window that I could not take my eyes off the view to let the words flow from my pen. At one point, near Hydrabad, I was writing in the middle of the night by the light of the burning ghats. The train was passing through the cremation grounds, and I could feel the heat of the burning bodies on my face.

For twenty-eight hours, I could not pull myself from that window. I saw beautifully ugly cities, where children played in mossy green temple tanks, some drawing drinking water in shining brass pots, and others doing their laundry, while a sadhu recited the Shiva Chalisa and bobbed up in prayer. I saw vast palaces, sprung from wealth beyond measure, which exhibited the most exquisite architecture I have ever seen, along with beautiful private pools and fountains, where peacocks displayed their plumage. And then, I would see a scene of utter and abject poverty: people and children in rags, scavenging through garbage cans, looking for food; and gypsies dancing and playing violin, with little trained monkeys scampering around them.

"At one point, the train came to a screeching halt. I fell out of my chair, and spilled onto the floor, laughing. When the belching black smoke from the engine cleared, I saw something from my window that I shall remember for the rest of my life. The first bright, red rays of dawn were blasting over the Western ghats. The bright reflection of the sun danced across each terraced rice paddy, like a dress covered with a thousand tiny mirrors where two mighty rivers converged into one dramatic, plummeting waterfall. At the base of these magnificent falls was a herd of nearly forty massive elephants, which were bathing and cavorting in the river. I sat in disbelief, rubbing my eyes to make sure I was not dreaming. This was my beloved India. This was a remarkable dream, a mystical vision, an unearthly beauty, for which, in all my world travels, I have never ever found an equal…"

India was such a dichotomy; such a collage of contrasting images of utter beauty and filth…the new, springing to life from the decaying ancient, like some antique creature trying to survive the modern world. I saw it all from my train window…birth and death; architectural wonders and

❄

starvation; a lonely Krishna playing flute amidst a flock of sheep; a huge Communist riot, with people being hit by clubs, and bleeding before my very eyes; a man holding a cobra as he waited to hop on the train; fields of elephants; jungles lit by evening fires and the distant roar of a tiger; and strangely surreal vendors, who would stick their hands through my train window at every stop, demanding bakshish.

This was the wonder that was India…image upon image flooded my mind, and at the end of my journey to Delhi, I felt that I deserved another Bachelor of Arts degree, just for surviving my train excursion.

I ran for my disappearing luggage again, and saw it promptly strapped to the back of a motorized rikshaw. The next thing I knew, I was speeding through Canaught Place — the Rodeo Drive of New Delhi —, and I believe we wiped out several bicyclists and a goat herd along the way. My taxi driver nipped one biker, sending him headlong into a bleeding collision with a tree. He sped on his merry way, as if this was an everyday occurrence. Life can be rather cheap in India.

I was on my way to visit my wonderful artistic friend, Madhoor Kapur, whose wealthy family lived in a palace in Chanakapuri, which is New Delhi's answer to Beverly Hills. Madhoor's mother met me at the door with a martini in hand, and I followed her through the long foyer, past exquisite murals her son had timelessly created on every wall. Mrs. Kapur was so fashionably thin, wrapped in a wonderful silk sari of golden mandalas, and she had those eyes that many Indian women have, so deeply upturned through worship and meditation that one rarely sees even the iris. She led me to a tower of the palace where Madhoor was painting, a marvelous studio of thick white Mogul minarets.

"You have come! And just in time for my art showing this evening. I am so happy to see you!"

My dear friend was covered in paint and surrounded by canvasses of very modern Indian art, and he was so dotted with color that he looked like he had been dancing in the Holi festival.

"Madhoor, I am going, you know…"

"Where?"

"To the Himalayas…"

"I was so hoping you would stay with me. You know you are welcome here, and I want to show you the cool side of New Delhi," Madhoor frowned.

❈

"My dear friend, I feel the call to the Himalayas. Something there is calling to me. I know not what or why…except that the call never stops."

"Then you must go…but tonight, you are mine. Get dressed! We have an art opening of mine to attend, and we are already late!"

I was once again speeding through the streets of New Delhi, this time on the back of Madhoor's Harley. We barely dodged a camel cart, only to come plowing into a flock of goats near the flower market. India was like an obstacle course, and we were weaving in and out of intersections where sacred cows had decided to bed down for the night, gently chewing hay and wreaking havoc to the traffic. One lady had parked her Mercedes, and was trying to lure the sacred bull out of the middle of the street with bananas. Horns were honking, dust was flying, and a huge truck of shudras in turbans splashed what appeared to be sewer water all over us at the traffic light. Madhoor only rolled his eyes and sailed on, with me hanging on for dear life!

The art opening was so fantastic. He had painted the most beautiful canvasses of flowing mauves and blue-grays, and somehow, subtly turned this all into likhit japa. As I moved in for a closer look, I saw that every canvas carried the most beautiful calligraphy of "RAMA," written in Devanagari. This went on from room to room. "Ram" was written everywhere, and there was a marvelous vibration among those of us who were experiencing the written sound of the Lord's name.

Later on, Madhoor took me to a very Bohemian discotheque to celebrate the evening's successes. I was shocked to see how modern India was, with girls in mini skirts and guys in black leather pants… everyone danced to the latest music from America. This was not particularly the India that was calling to me. I was a man on a mission, and nothing could take me from my inner call.

the call of the ganga

I headed the next morning to Rishikesh by taxi, which drove along the Ganges, and I was thrilled. The Ganges was everything I thought it would be. The closer I got to the magnificent river, the more I could actually hear music coming from it. For me, it was a sound like a symphony...I could hear the most magnificent strains of music emanating from the water, and at the same time, I heard voices. There were thousands of voices inside the river: a symphony of stories, songs, and cries of ecstacy; and stories of joy, pain, sorrow, and exaltations. All of life was contained within that river. I have traveled on every continent on this planet, and I can forcefully say that there is NO OTHER river on this planet like the Ganges.

❖

Finally, upon arriving in Rishikesh, I found that I must trek further to reach the Sivananda Ashram, which was my destination. For the final leg of my journey, I found myself piling into the most delightful gypsy pony. Hearing the pony bells in the cool Himalayan air, alongside the roar of the Ganges, made me want to sing "Sleigh Ride." I was delighted to be in Rishikesh. After New Delhi, the mountains were so refreshing. Here, everyone appeared to be a swami! Everyone was in ochre dhotis, and seemed to be walking about, singing, "Sita Ram!" We would pass sadhus and naga babas, with their massive jatas wound high upon their heads; each wore only a trisula as they passed down the dark country roads. The steady clang of temple bells could be heard, and I looked through doorways to see the waving of arati lamps.

"Sahib, you are here, and it is time for prayers!" I was hustled down from the gypsy cart and quickly had my feet washed, and then rushed to the darshan hall. A beautiful murti of Lord Subramaniya was the object of worship, and was in the process of being covered with flowers. In the background, all the monks were singing, "Subramanium, Subramanium, Subramanium Parhimam!" Conches were being blown, Ganges water was being thrown on us, arati lights were being waved, incense was glowing, and the chief pujari was fanning the deity with a chori yak tail whisk. The smile on my face was infinite. I was in my element, and my heart spilled over with bhava and happiness to have arrived at such a place.

A secretary of Swami Chidananda's was apologizing to me that they had run out of rooms and had given my reserved room to a female brahmachari. He said that he could only give me accommodations in the hall of swamis, which was built out over the Ganges with the mighty river flowing below it. I told him that I would be happy to stay in the hall of swamis.

"But Sir, you will have to sleep on the hard cold stone floor. You are wearing only a thin khourta, and it is cold here at night. Perhaps we can call a taxi and send you to a hotel."

I shook my head and said with determination, "Absolutely NOT!" I was happy to head for the cold stone floor, and the opportunity to absorb the atmosphere of bhakti surrounding the swamis. As I looked about the room at the aging swamis, some with long white beards and yards of dreadlocks, and others with shaved heads and severely thin bodies, I felt so honored to be in this crew of Sivanandaites. I went to the window, watched the moon rise over the foothills of the Himalayas and dance across the sparkling holy waters of the Ganges, and I wrote in my journal:

"There is within my heart a secret door,
A door that at your touch will softly swing,
And bid you dance across a moonswept floor
And your heart into the Starbright Stillness
Soar…"

"You write beautifully…" a voice echoed in my soul. It was a voice that I immediately recognized and loved. I looked up into the eyes of the old Swami, who was reading my journal over my shoulder. My heart melted as I looked into those kind and wise eyes. I felt that a huge leg of my journey was over, and that I wanted to touch this stranger's feet. He had the warmest smile I had ever seen in my life. He looked at my face as if he were seeing an old friend, and I saw a crystal tear form in the corner of his right eye.

"I am Swami Shankarananda Giri."

"I am…"

"It's okay; I know who you are."

"You do?"

"Oh yes, I have been waiting for you for years." Swami Shankarananda's smile beamed at me, and I felt surrounded by an ocean of peace. He led me to his place of rest and offered me his humble bed. I flatly refused, and said I should be helping him to bed.

Swami said, "You shoulder hurts; did you injure it?"

I was astonished. I thought, "this guy reads minds, too!" I nodded my head yes.

He produced a bottle of Aruyvedic oil, and started massaging my shoulder. Within minutes, the pain had subsided, and he created a beautiful pallet for me to sleep on. This was a huge luxury for a man with only a dhoti, no pillow, and no blanket. I knelt, thanked Lord Shiva for my good fortune, and lay down to sleep to the melodic sound coming from Swamiji's sleep.

That night, I dreamed again of the beautiful woman with long black hair. "Are you here my son? Have you come to India to see me?" She smiled so radiantly, and there was a golden crown on Her head, with a lotus just above Her third eye. She gave me a dunda, and we walked a long walk up a hill in massive jungle. At the top clearing, She showed me the beautiful lands below, and I could see the meandering path of the Ganges flowing below, but here it was a small young river. "This, my son, is the promised land…"

❖

I awoke, and the swamis were stirring for their morning bath in Ganges. It was around 4:00 a.m., and it was cold. I wasn't about to miss this chance for my first morning dip in my sacred river, and Swamiji was already up and ready to go! We laughed, and he held my hand as we rushed down the path in the dark, towards the raging rapids.

"Be careful, and don't venture out too far into the middle of the Ganges. The current is very strong here, and some have been swept away..."

I so appreciated his care, and followed his every instruction. We bathed, and Swamiji taught me to chant "Om Wak, Om Pran, Om Shakshu, Om Strotam, Om Shira, Om Hridayam..." as he placed Ganga water on my mouth, my nose, my eyes, my ears, my mind, and my heart, respectively.

photo by Krishna Priya

"Om Shanti, Shanti, Shantahi...Jai!" It was like bathing in ice water, and I loved it. I had never been touched by anything so magical as that first dip in the Ganges. I knew immediately why this river is sacred, and I felt at once cleansed and invigorated.

We put on fresh dhotis, and headed back up the embankment. On a large rock slab overlooking Shivananda ghat, Swamiji instructed me in morning Ashtanga Yoga postures and cleansings. He taught me jala neti, the cleansing of the nose with an old clay water pot, and he started my instruction in Pranayama, Hatha, and Karma Yoga.

I felt so fortunate to have just arrived, and to already be under the tutelage of a swami. It seemed to me that this was all the grace of Lord Shiva as Ashutosh, and was the fulfillment of all my dreams and desires. Before I could say anything, Swamiji read my mind, and said, "Yes, this grace is from Lord Shiva, for all your years of devotion. Shiva is the kindest God. You are a very fortunate young man."

I looked up at my fearless teacher, who was always smiling and laughing. I started to wonder if this aged swami was not a form of Lord Shiva himself. The yoga class was wonderful, and my heart was elated to be doing asanansa on a great stone cliff overlooking the Ganga. Yoga made so very much sense in this atmosphere! Swamiji paid so much attention to my every move, correcting me here and there, and re-demonstrating each pose until I had it perfectly. He was incredibly agile for his age, for any age...he appeared ageless and handsome, with glowing skin.

He taught me how to properly wrap my dhoti, and we headed off arm in arm for breakfast at the banquet hall. All of the Swamis chimed in singing the mahamantram: "Om Trayambikum, Ya Chamahe... I loved the way the Sivananda swamis sang this great chant to Shiva, asking for moksha..."Just as the cucumber is severed from the vine, release me from this endless cycle of rebirth, Lord Shiva." The food at Sivananda ashram is very simple and very pure.

Afterwards, we did some seva, cleaning brush in the ashram yard. I was happy to render selfless service for such a rich order of swamis. As I worked, I watched two beige monkeys sneak down the side of a wall and onto the balcony of an unsuspecting English woman's apartment. They entered her apartment, where she was nervously wrapping a sari, and they scandalously stole an entire bowl of oranges! The English lady ran to the balcony, and with clenched fist, gave them a huge verbal beating. The monkeys responded by chattering back at her with raised oranges, and bulged out their lips in a horrid imitation of the lady. Swamiji and I sat down our rakes, and roared with laughter!

After a short nap, he took me across the Ganges for the first time to visit a great saint living in a cave there. His name was the Maharishi Mahesh Yogi. At that time, no one knew of Maharishi, and he was a simple saint meditating in a cave. This was before the Beatles, before Mia Farrow, and before Transcendental Meditation. He was a very short man with a huge personality! I so enjoyed meditating with him, as he had built an underground chamber for meditation, which was very, very quiet. I meditated with Maharishi for nearly an hour…it was a very still, peaceful, and powerful shakti. At the end of the meditation, he gave me a flower and a small gold locket with his picture on it, which I wear to this day. He blessed me, and told Swamiji that I would become a great Sannyasin.

On the way back from visiting Maharishi, Swamiji and I played in the forest. He would jump on a huge rock, beating his chest and roaring with laughter, and tell me he was Hanuman! Swamiji never stopped laughing. He was the happiest man I had ever known. I told Swamiji that if he was Hanuman, I certainly was NOT Ravana! Then he proceeded to jump down on top of me and tell me I would be burned by his tail. Every day we were clowning like this, and I was thrilled to touch and grapple with such a holy man. I realized that this play was all just his way of giving me constant shaktipa.

On the ferry boat back across the Ganges, the pilgrims were all singing, "Ganga Ma Ki Jai," and throwing money into the water. I could not believe I was living in such a magical place. Everywhere Swamiji and I went, there was laughter, intense devotion, and swamis everywhere, singing, "Jai Sita Ram." It was the standard for the holy land in which I was living.

Every moment of living next to the Ganges was charged. Everyone I met appeared to be a saint. I know this sounds idealized, but this is exactly the way Rishikesh appeared to be, to me, in the 1960's. It was pure, unspoiled, spiritual India; an India relatively undiscovered by the West, and mostly forgotten by the Indians. The sadhus and swamis had full run of this area, and it was land specifically set aside for ashrams, spiritual studies, hermitages; a place for sadhus to live alone in caves. I kept pinching myself, thinking I would wake up from this dream…but it was not a dream; it was the India I truly loved.

The daily regimen at the ashram was always the same, day after day, and yet the dance of newcomers was welcomed, which added a note of drama. In the morning was ritual bathing in Ganges at 4:00 a.m.; then manglarati and meditation; puja; yoga practice, and breakfast. Afternoon was nap, or free time to travel and meet saints; then, it was time to do Karma Yoga, seva, or tiffin. Later, we were able to study independently; or take a nap. Then, it was time to dress for dinner; do kirtan; eat dinner; and perform evening puja and kirtana. This was the same schedule, day after day, week after week. What made it so unique was that each afternoon, Swamiji and I would go visit another saint. Some days, we found our way to the beautiful Tat Wala Baba, who sat naked, with jatas touching the floor. His body was so beautiful and glowing, like the body of a fifteen-year-old, yet I knew he was in his sixties. He was a stunning lecturer on yoga, and lived in a cave with his cat. I went to see him nearly every day to take his darshan, and to just sit quietly with him in meditation. Finally, he invited me to stay in his cave, and I passed a couple of nights there. It was exquisite to stay near Tat Wala Baba, and at night, there seemed to be numerous wild animals coming through the doorway. Cave life in India is very, very rigorous. Tat Wala Baba had his life totally refined, and he lived so beautifully, an exquisite man with a marvelous physique, deep spirituality, and a powerful aura.

adventures with swamiji

One day, Swamiji and I climbed high up on a ledge above the Ganges, where we scaled the hill wall nearly two hundred feet. As we neared the top, I heard a plink-plink sound coming from a cave. Swamiji called out "Rosie!" to the occupant, and out came a wild-looking woman. She was dressed in animal skins, had dreadlocks piled on the top of her head, and carried a trident! She looked like a female version of Lord Shiva! This woman was of German descent, and she had been in this cave for many years. When we investigated more carefully, we discovered that the plink-plink sound was coming from a sculpture she was working on. She had carved beautiful, life-sized murtis of many gods and goddesses. Her work was elaborately carved into white marble, and looked a bit like Raphael.

Swami Shankarananda Giri was a very high swami, and was respected by so many saints in the Himalayas. Everywhere he went, he was known by everyone, and people like the Maharishi regarded him as an old friend. He took me to meet so many babas, most of them completely unknown and reclusive. Normally, they would not receive visitors. I was so blessed to take the darshan of so many saints, babas, naga babas and gurus. Some would bring out treatises for me to read, which were much like Ph.D. theses on one subject or another, all of them focused on spiritual inquiry and sadhana. Some of these manuscripts represented a yogi's entire life work. I wish I could have copied each one on the spot, but instead, I would speed read everything, and record it in my heart.

One swami, Nirgunananda Giri, had written a remarkable work on Svara Yoga, or the synchronicity between the cycles of sleep and nostril alternation during the night. He suggested that nightmares occur more easily when a subject is sleeping on their left side. His work suggested that a yogi should always sleep on their right side to have less pressure on the heart, and stressed the importance of keeping both nostrils equally open during the night, in order to create more balance and mastery over the mind.

I learned so much during this time period that I cannot even fathom what these great babas taught me. One baba handed me a paper that read, "How to prove the existence of God to a resistant student." I read that and tried all the techniques, and they were incredible! This man had spent some sixty years working on this technique and writing the paper that he showed me. He was quite old. As far as I know, the work was never published when he left his body. Perhaps I am one of the few people on this planet to be privy to his years of sadhana, and the techniques he developed for spiritual realization.

Swami Shankarananda Giri made sure that every teacher he knew spent time with me. I had no idea why I was the center of so much kindness and attention from the sadhus…I could only be grateful to the supreme Lord for so much kindness in educating a lowly child like me!

The pujas at Sivananda Ashram were inspiring, and would feature a different deity each night. I loved the spirited kirtan and the holy atmosphere of the ashram. Most of all, I loved sleeping in the swami hall and soaking in, all night long, such powerful shakti from some of India's greatest living swamis at that time. Swami Shankarananda took such care with me, as if he were caring for his own son. He rubbed my back every night, and rubbed my feet with special oils. I wanted to rub his feet, for I felt that was my position as Shesha, but he wouldn't allow it. He was always happy, and always laughing in bliss, almost every second of every day. He was always joking with me, hitting me on the back, and hugging me. I felt so touched by his shakti, and it was overwhelming to experience such a surge of constant kindness. These were the qualities of a true saint…bliss and kindness.

During the day, we would sit on big rocks on the Ganges, and he would read me passages from the *Ramayana*; a dissertation on the *Bhagavad Gita*; the *Puranas*; the *Isha* and *Kena Upanishad*; and then narrate the entire *Mahabharata* to me. These works contain the basis of Hindu scriptures and mythology. He particularly took his time explaining to me in detail the message of Sri Krishna in the *Bhagavad Gita*, where Lord Krishna tells us that we should not grieve if we face death. Krishna says we lose our body just as if we were taking off a worn-out garment, and that we put on a new body just as if we were putting on new cothes. He explained to me that we are eternal and infinite beings, and that death is the greatest lie. Our soul, our spirit, is divine and immortal.

There is nothing greater in life than having a wonderful swami teach you as you sit with him under a tree on the banks of the Ganges River. It is the perfect atmosphere for understanding. Swamiji would look endearingly into my eyes, the Ganga dancing through bright rapids at his side. The smell of sweet jasmine incense would swirl on a temple breeze, and he would read to me from the Isha Upanishad, singing the words:

"A hard diamond crust hides that Self (of man). O thou Truth remove my own veil and show me Thy face in me! O Thou the nourisher, supreme seer, shining in all, and the sun, gather thy rays, withdraw thy lustrous fire so that I can see thy face. All that is, is One; that One I am. This body ends in ashes; the breathless life goes to deathlessness. O my mind, call to memory all that thou hast done. O thou fire, lead us to true position by the right path."

My education never stopped. Swamiji had a way of teaching that left the message written on my Soul. Then, he would say, laughing…

"Have you ever been to the temple of one thousand Shivas?"

"Swamiji of course not, I have never been to Rishikesh before…"

"Oh yes, you have; you just can't remember yet. Come, let's go!"

And we would be off on another adventure, crossing a rope bridge over a perilous Ganges waterfall; trekking through a jungle; climbing over boulders and sneaking around big baboons; and finally, ending up at a small temple built over a waterfall, where, due to trick mirrors, Shiva would appear over a thousand times in each direction, painted in dayglow colors and displayed under a black light, and wearing a wig of real human hair! I would just stand there, amazed at the colors, the audacity, and the shakti…

❊

The living regimen in an Indian ashram is pretty much the same day in and day out. We awoke at 4:00 a.m.; took our cold plunge into the raging Ganges; did our morning ablutions; dressed and shaved our heads; did puja and kirtana as the sun rose; and performed a nice, long meditation as the first rays of sun danced across the waves of the Ganges. All of this was followed by an hour of rigorous Ashtanga on the bank of the river. For some Americans, starting out the day with such structure was hell, and they got on the first airplane home! For me, this lifestyle was heaven. It made sadhana easy. I could feel Swami Sivananada's hand everywhere, designing the perfect environment in which to realize God. He said, "Set up your regime. Don't miss a beat. Sing to God all day long with ecstacy. Perform your puja, japa, and asana. Chant as you offer seva. Keep your mind ever on the goal of Self Realization…" Everything at the ashram was constructed toward achieving this goal, in the glorious setting in the foothills of the Himalayas along the gentle banks of the Ganga. I noticed that a smile was being permanently placed on my face. It was a genuine smile, which came from a glowing heart. It felt so good to smile that smile. I lived every day to feel that smile on my young face…

I thought I would live this lifestyle with Swami Shankarananda Giri forever…and I hoped only to continue on with each day of worship, karma yoga, and our adventures. We do not see change coming, and we cannot anticipate the ways of an enlightened being. Sometimes, in order to teach us, they will shock us with their inconsistency. Perhaps the greatest naivete is the thought that somehow, when we have found happiness in this world, that this transitory world will not change. But the fact is, everyone and everything are constantly changing. You had better hang loose, with non-attachment, or you will suffer.

One afternoon, Swamiji and I were walking along the Ganges, and I noticed that he was looking lingeringly at me. The look in his eyes was so thoughtful, so full of unconditional love. He beckoned to me to sit on a large rock, where we both assumed lotus position across from each other. The smile on my face could not have been more blissful; happiness danced in my heart, and I lived on each wave of shakti coming from such a holy being.

"You know I am going away. My work is done. Now, I think it is time for me to leave my body…" I blinked, and looked at my dear teacher incredulously. I could feel my smile fade, and warm tears started to stream down my face. How could such a positive person of sunlight and love say such things?

"Swamiji, no, please don't speak this way…" I had found happiness, and I didn't want my world to crumble before my very eyes. "I am far from being finished. Please, Swamiji, you cannot leave me and this world. We both need your enlightened teaching…" I could only think of so many people in the West alone who would benefit from Swami's great teachings. He had a huge following in India in Andra Pradesh, where his ashram was, along with a huge following at his ashrams in South Africa and Fiji.

"I can only think that it is time for me to walk to Benares, and prepare to leave my body. Don't think of death as a bad thing. I am old, and I have taught you all that I know. My teaching will live on in you, and now I have a dharma successor. I am free to go be with Shiva…"

"But Swamiji," I said, now truly fighting back tears. "I know so very little. I couldn't possibly be worthy enough to be your dharma successor. I am just a teenage boy with so little experience. Please, Swamji, don't joke with me this way…"

"I have been the 147th Jagad Guru of the Adi Parashakti Shiva Peetham, and now you will be the 148th. Now you know the way…and I would not have chosen you if it wasn't right. I knew who you were from the moment I met you. You are a very old soul, and you are not new to me. I remembered you from this very lifetime."

"Swamiji, do you mean I lived in India in my previous life, and that you knew me?"

"Yes." He looked away at the ever-flowing Ganges.

"Who was I? Can you tell me?"

"That will all be revealed to you in time."

"Swamiji, please do not tell me you are going to walk on to Benares without me. If you are planning to die, then let me tend to you and take care of you. I do not want you to do this alone. I will be by your side until your last breath…it is the dharma of a son to care for his father this way. You are my true holy father."

"No, my child, a sadhu must face these things alone. I feel I must go on to Benares alone."

"But walking, Swamiji…you have no shoes."

Swamiji looked down at his worn and chaffed feet.

"I owe you so much," I said, with tears streaming down my face." I owe you my life…what you have done for me has changed my entire life. At least, Swamiji, allow me to buy you a pair of chappals for your journey."

He nodded, and we walked silently to the bazaar. The smile I loved to feel so on my face had faded. How could it come so quickly and go? I started to feel in my heart the caution of Sri Aurobindo when he said, "Beware of the valley of the false enlightenment. You think that you are really there, but it is a false glimmer and you have miles to go." I was attached to my happiness, and I was shaken to my foundations. How could my beloved teacher leave me after so many months of sadhana and satsang together? Particularly, it had been my hope that we would be together to our last breath. How could he even tell me he was contemplating death? This was more than my young mind could grasp.

When we got to the bazaar, I had Swamiji's foot measured in sand. After the imprint was made, I asked to have some of the sand back, and I placed it in a bag. As they made the chappals, Swami sat in a chair, and I sat on the floor beside him, with a bowed head. He had his hand on the top of my head and was chanting "Rama, Rama, Rama, Rama, Rama…ad infinitum." I was fighting back tears of disbelief, and feeling helpless to change his mind. The chappals were finished, and they were so beautiful, the finest in all of Rishikesh. I had performed puja to Swamiji's feet, and had washed them in fresh Ganges water…and I drank some of the water which had touched his feet. He looked down at me with such overwhelming love that I felt that the top of my head was burning. I annointed his feet with sandalwood oil, and placed the new shoes on his feet.

Swamiji was smiling at me, with the most beautiful smile, and laughing. I kept waiting for him to tell me this was a joke…just a ploy to get new sandals. It didn't happen. When he stood up and looked in the mirror at his beautiful new chappals, he said, "Now I know what it feels like to be a millionaire!" I laughed and shook my head, and silently said to myself, "I hope I shall always be so simple that a new pair of sandals will make me feel like a millionaire."

I grabbed some fruit and supplies in the marketplace for Swamiji's journey, and wrapped them in a small satchel. I felt that I owed this man my life, and that these small things were the least I could do. In India, you treat your teacher like a king, like God. You do everything you can for your teacher, without a thought of cost, and as selflessly as possible, like drinking the water in which you have bathed his feet. These things are all very high blessings, or ashirba from the guru. I tried to hide three hundred rupees in his satchel, but Swamiji caught me, and returned the money.

We walked to the edge of Rishikesh, holding hands, and there, he was determined to walk the dusty road to Benares. In India, Benares is considered to be the ideal place to die. Shiva has promised that anyone who dies in Benares shall have eternal life in him, as well as moksha. Swamiji embraced me and asked me not to be so brokenhearted. He said for me to be happy for him, and that I now needed to be open to new teachings. I thought that he was implying that a new teacher was coming into my life…but how could that be? Swamiji was my teacher. He embraced me and gave me a secret mantra, which I was never to share with another soul. He told me how happy he was for me, and he kissed me on the forehead.

I stood with my hands in pranam, watching him walk down the road until his thin body disappeared on the horizon. I thought, "There walks a Godman, maybe even Shiva himself!" I gave prayers of thanks to God for sending me Swamiji, and for everything that he had taught me: for all the people he had introduced me to; for all the teachings of other saints he had shared with me; and for my vast education over the past eight months, scripturally, as well as in daily experience.

I was stunned, and in a state of shock as well. I felt as if the most important person in my life had died, and I was deeply grieving being apart from my teacher. I kept chanting the mantra he had given me, and I walked right past the ashram, and sat on the banks of the Ganges all night long in a remote place where the river was very peaceful.

The next morning, I headed out for the forest. My mantra was ever on my lips. I noticed how green and beautiful everything was, and how even the flowers seemed to be glowing. I passed a Tibetan relocation area, where a great deal of chanting was coming from the Lamasary. I love Tibetan chanting, and several young monks saw me listening at the door and invited me in. A great lama had died, and they were performing the seven-day funeral chant. It was at a very low pitch, with cymbals and huge, twenty-foot horns being blown. The sound was so surreal and so charged that it actually brought some solace to my soul. I spent several nights chanting with them, and the monks gave me a place to sleep in the dharmasala. I found the Tibetans to be so kind and so industrious. After China had crushed them out of their own country, they had resettled in India so perfectly, recreating their own culture in just a short time.

I wandered in the forest outside the lamasary each day, and met many sadhus living there near Dera Dune. I knew one baba, who took me in, and we sat smoking chillam and chanting "OM Nama Shivaya." He was a naga baba, and he encouraged me to leave behind my dhoti, stop shaving my head, and just chant to Shiva. He gave me the trisula that had belonged to a sadhu friend of his who had gone higher up into the Himalayas to live. How my life had changed from being with Swamiji at the ashram…now, I was in rags, chanting around a fire and carrying a massive iron trident, covered in ash and smoking chillam. My weight had dropped in a month to one hundred five pounds, and for a six-foot frame, that was very thin. My skin had become brown and cracked from the sun, and my feet were blistered from walking everywhere. I really didn't care much for myself anymore, and was searching instead for that elusive smile that used to feel so good on my face. Would I ever find that smile again?

I carried a picture of Swamiji in my bead bag, and I prayed for him three times a day. The rest of the time, Sadbari Baba and I chanted to Lord Shiva. I prayed that Lord Shiva would cause a miracle so that Swamiji would come back to me, and that we would pick up our lives and teaching where we left off. Babaji cautioned me not to become attached to gurus or saints, because, he said, "They come and go like the wind. They live on many planes simultaneously. No one can hold them, and they move with freedom everywhere in the universe. To love such a person is like loving the wind…but how shall you catch the wind?" What he said made sense to me, and he encouraged me to be a sadhu, and to live strongly and reclusively like him. He sat for many hours in meditation, and he was so grounded that it was like being near a giant tree.

Sadbari Baba asked me to collect some wood in the forest, so that we could do a yagna. I went walking in the dark without shoes or clothes. I was now quite scruffy, with long hair and beard, and a very, very thin and tanned body from living outdoors. I had lost all fear even of the fierce animals that shared the forest with us. That night, I collected wood pieces by starlight, and looked above the tall trees to see a nighttime canopy of myriad stars. I also felt as if I was being watched by a thousand small eyes. I knew that the animals were watching me collect wood, and that they regarded me as a brother of the forest. I brought the wood back, and Sadbari Baba created a beautiful fire. He was pouring ghee, placing incense into the fire, and chanting the 1,008 names of Lord Shiva.

It was a powerful yagna. Sitting across from him, I watched the firelight dance across the face of the sadhu, his jattas touching the ground. His face transformed from that of a handsome young man into a fierce creature, and then into a benign face much like Shiva's. I watched him age, grow young, become haggard, and then look like Buddha, all within a space of a few hours. I realized that this young man was living simultaneously in many worlds. Just being near such a sadhu is a great boon. I was sure Swamiji was pulling strings to make this all happen, and that he was still teaching me, though he was far away. It was wonderful, because I no longer felt abandoned, and I realized that my spiritual education was continuing.

That night, I fell asleep by the light of Babaji's fire. I remember looking up at the stars and listening to his chanting…and suddenly, I saw the approach of an eerie figure. It was the beautiful Indian woman, with the long, flowing, black hair, from my dreams. She said, "Is that really you? You have come to me?" Then, She faded away. I awoke the next morning, and Babaji was gone. I arose, and started walking in the forest.

mother's great lila

I noticed that the flowers of the forest had gotten brighter. The colors of the small flowers I was picking were purple and bright gold, and were touched with saffron. They were shaped just like mandalas, and actually seemed to be transforming before my eyes. I could see the mandalas swirling, and I started to wonder what they had put in my chai! The whole forest started to glow around me. I wasn't sure why I was picking this bouquet of flowers, but the flowers were all taking on the shapes of mandalas, and some were actually swirling in my hands, like chakras.

I decided that this was an enchanted forest, and I came to the realization that this was a forest where Sita and Lord Rama had actually stayed when they were in exile. I could feel their

❁

31

energy, and I started to sweetly sing, "Sita Ram, Sita Ram, Ragupathi Ragava Raja Ram!" The flowers, the glowing forest, and the enchantment were now dancing all around me...I seriously started to question my sanity. I had not eaten a good meal for weeks, only a little bit of milk each day. Maybe this was the hallucination that went hand in hand with starvation. But it was ecstatic, and I felt my lips, and there, once again, was my wonderful smile. Ah yes, I had found it again! I looked at the glowing flowers I was picking, and felt Sita and Rama all around me and I started to weep tears of joy. "God, you haven't deserted me, only I was too blind to know your ways..."

Just then, I spotted an old Packard car, bouncing its way through the forest. The road was horrible! It was filled with chug holes, and this car was bouncing wildly...it was a shocking jungle sight, because I had not seen a vehicle of any kind in weeks. This was a remote place in the forest, and I was astonished to see this car! Furthermore, the outside of the car was draped with marigolds. It looked so beautiful, like a moving altar. The car approached slowly, looking like a bobbing boat on a choppy sea. It was making a beeline right for me! I moved to the side of the road, holding my bouquet of flowers and looking like such a sight...with my rags, beard, dreadlocks, and the broken, parched skin of a brown forest samana. The car stopped right next to me, and the back window went down.

There, to my astonishment, sat the woman of my dreams. It was Her Face! I felt cold chills running up and down my body. I was shaking and starting to cry. The woman was in a state of ecstasy. She was excited and smiling, as if she was seeing an old friend after a long time. She was looking at me, and crying, "Ram, Ram, Ram, Ram," with a look of recognition on her face! I had never heard or seen anyone in my life exclaim something with so much bhava. The woman sitting next to Her started speaking to me in a heavy Indian accent. "Listen. The Divine Mother is speaking to you!" I listened, intently pressing my face closer to Hers, and I accidentally dropped my bouquet of flowers. They fell directly on Her feet inside the car. She exclaimed, "Ram, Ram, Ram, Ram," again, in a high, ecstatic state. I was not sure if the car could contain such a woman. It seemed like the shakti was so strong that the vehicle would just explode.

I was now certain that I had lost my mind completely. This was exactly the woman from my dreams! This was the woman I had been dreaming about since the age of ten. This was the

❖

woman who had told me that She was my Mother, and to come to India. Surely, this was some type of delusion from malnutrition; surely, I was hallucinating. Once again, the lady in the car chided me, "MA is speaking to you; will you please just listen?"

"What is She saying?"

"She said that your name is Ramananda. Now, get in the car!"

The party made room for me in the front seat, and I climbed in. There was so much electricity in the car that I felt immobilized. There was light running up and down the back of my spine, and I was tingling all over. I had never felt anything like this in my entire life. I could feel the strongest presence behind me, and with all my heart I wanted to turn around and look at the woman behind me, the beautiful woman of my dreams. I finally garnered all of my courage, and turned around to look at Her. To my astonishment, I could see Her body in a white robe, with a yellow towel on Her head…but under the towel, there was no face — only light streaming out at me, nearly blinding me. I decided that I had best not look behind me anymore! The man in the front seat said, "Babuji, this is Sri Sri Anandamayi MA."

I turned around to say, "Namaste MA," and She was now in a very removed state of bhava. From the formation of Her mouth, I could see that She was obviously chanting RAM, except that now, no sound was coming out. Her head was waving wildly as She formed the words RAM, but there was absolutely no sound. I had never seen anyone chant with such fervor, and never have I since seen anyone in such a state of bliss. I will never forget what Mother looked like as She chanted, "Ram, Ram, Ram…" with no sound emanating from Her lips. She smiled so sweetly at me that I could not keep the tears from falling from my eyes. I looked back at Her, and in my mind I said, "It is really you!" She nodded, smiling, as if She heard my every thought.

Then, MA started talking to the driver of the car in the sweetest voice, just like a little girl. He started to translate for me:

"We are on our way to Swami Ram Tirth Ashram in Rajport. MA requests that you go with us there."

"Okay, fine."

"MA says you are Ramananda."

"Whoever MA says I am, I am. Tell Mother I have been dreaming of Her for years."

He spoke to Mother, and I heard Her say, "of course."

Then, through Dr. Patel, Mother explained: "There was a young sadhu who lived very close to my ashram in Benares. He was Ramananda. He was the Guru to Kabir. Kabir always used to watch him walk to the Ganges each day to bathe. One day, he stepped on Kabir's hand; Kabir obtained shaktipa, and he became a devotee immediately. I told everyone that one day, Ramananda would return. And here he sits, as a boy in the front seat."

There was a sigh from Udas sitting in the back. Suddenly, the Indians started treating me differently. I went from being treated like a tramp to gaining the respect of a holy man. I looked smilingly back at MA, but there was no face under the towel…only an empty space where the towel should be. I winced, and just quietly said, "Jai MA."

When we arrived at the ashram, I ran out of the car and fell at Mother's feet. She stood near me for a long time, and I looked at Her lovely, tiny feet. I wished so in my heart that I had a flower garland to offer Her, so I offered Her instead a mansika puja of a thousand garlands with my mind.

I did not care about who or what I had been in a past life. I knew only I wanted to worship at Her feet and be Her servant for my entire life. Mother moved on in Her quiet gliding way, as if Her feet barely touched the ground. I was taken away to the glass house for a shower and a shave, and was given fresh clothes to wear. I went to my room, and it was so wonderful and clean after living and sleeping on the ground in a sadhu camp. I sat in quiet meditation, reflecting on the day's events, and writing like crazy in my journal:

"Today, I FOUND HER, the woman of my dreams. She has been coming to me since I was ten years old, saying, 'I am your Mother. Come to India.' Now, I know that She exists, and that She is Sri Sri Anandamayi Ma. She is even more lovely than in my dreams, and is older now. Though Her face is that of a woman in her seventies, Her spirit is eternal. I have never looked upon such sweet eyes in my life. What I experienced in the car left no doubt in my mind. She was glowing as She appeared and disappeared at will and flowed from one ecstatic state to another; the energy has left me nearly unable to walk. I cannot even remember where I have been for the last three days, as my mind is staggering so much under the shakti. There is no doubt in my mind that if anyone in India has achieved enlightenment, Anandamayi MA is there. As far as I am concerned, SHE IS GOD."

There was a quiet knock on my door. "Mother will see you now." I hurried down the back stairs, and was taken to a small cottage, where the name "MA" had been written with marigolds

❖

in Sanskrit on the trellis outside. I walked in and did full pranam on the floor before Her. Mother was dressed in a simple white sheet, with a yellow towel draped around her neck. Her hair was coiled up on Her head in an ushnisha, making Her look so much like Buddha to me, for some reason.

She smiled at me so sweetly, and waved her head back and forth as she looked at me and said, "Acha, Acha." Through the interpreter, She spoke to me:

"Are you comfortable?"

"Yes, MA, I am very comfortable. Thank you for rescuing me!"

Mother threw Her head back and laughed.

"Did I rescue you, Ramananda. From what?"

"From life."

Mother laughed loudly.

"I did not rescue you from life. I am here to involve you in your sadhanna."

"And for that dear MA, I am eternally grateful. Thank you so much." I could feel warm tears streaming down my face, but I maintained control, and smiled back at my beautiful teacher.

"What were you doing in the forest?" She smiled and lifted her eyebrows.

"Mother, I was picking flowers and thinking of Sita and Ram living in such a forest."

MA smiled, and nodded to the other people in the room, and they all smiled back at me, shaking their heads sideways.

"MA, you have been coming to me in my dreams since I was just a child. I have come all the way from America to find a meaning to those dreams, and I did not even know you existed. Now, I am home, and the greatest hope in my heart is to take initiation with you and to spend the rest of my life at your Lotus Feet." I looked up at Mother's face, and She started to glow in the most incredible way. It was as if She had flipped a switch and a huge nuclear power plant had engaged a light, which emanated from Her body. My body was shaken to its very core, and there was a huge pressure on the top of my head. Tears were streaming down my face as I looked at Her, because what I saw was the power of pure DIVINE LOVE. I had never been loved to this degree in my life.

Mother sat very still, and the light continued to grow. Now, there was a visible glow around Her whole body. The Indian women in the room were ahhhing and sighing, and also seemed to be seeing what I was seeing. I felt such a rush of energy through the top of my head that I was not sure if I could contain such shakti. Mother's face was radiant, and she was in an obvious state of ecstasy. For a moment, She held me in that ecstasy, and I was completely out of space-time continuum; I was tasting eternity and heaven all at once. I could feel tears falling from my eyes, but I wasn't in any way sad. I was laughing for joy…because I realized that everything in life is true; that a boy could have a dream, and that a dream is in fact a call to a higher reality. I realized that God really did exist, and that She cared enough to call me across the planet to the other side of the world to make sure I knew of Her love. There was a golden circle of light completely around MA's body, and She folded Her hands into pranam, and She continued to smile and pranam to me. The light was nearly blinding, as if She were floating in a big bubble of light. I blinked several times to see if I was hallucinating, but such a miracle truly was unfolding before my very eyes. Then, as sweetly as this had occurred, the light obtained a softer glow around MA. The energy in the room became softer and more subtle, and I was left sitting at Her Lotus Feet, visibly shaking.

The day I met my Guru was the day I had lived for all my life. I stretched out in a full pranam before MA, and in my heart, I said over and over, "Please take me, I am yours." In my mind, I could only see myself hanging onto Her ankles for dear life. But then, an incredible feeling of peace swept over me, and I felt as if She was cleaning me. I suddenly felt so light, so changed, and so happy. I had taken a huge dump of my "stuff," and suddenly, I couldn't remember any hardship in life. I felt light, I felt free, and I was in a mystical state of bliss.

"Shukria MA, Shukria…" Finally, the devotees helped me stand. I was ushered out of the room, and only stopped at the door to look back. MA still sat there on Her cot, radiantly glowing. The expression on Her face was more beautiful than that of any Madonna I had ever seen painted. I prayed to Shiva that I would always be able to remember this experience, and that I would remember Her face just that way. The devotees told me to take food…but I really just wanted to go to my room and write.

They insisted that I needed food, so I was led to the banquet hall and given a huge plate of rice and delicious subjis. It is hard to fully appreciate food after you have been blown into the fifth dimension. Honestly, I was struggling even to remember my name, and even that name had no more meaning for me. From that moment on, I knew that I could only be Ramananda, and anything of my past was past.

After my meal, I was sent to bed. I could hear kirtan coming from the satsang hall. "Sri Krishna, Govina, Hare Murare…" was sifting through my mind as I fell into the most satisfying sleep of my life. I was completely at peace, and with my Mother, like a newborn baby. I awoke pinching myself, still unable to believe my good fortune and incredible experiences with MA.

I stayed at Swami Ram Tirth Ashram in Rajport for nearly a week, and enjoyed the lovely spiritual atmosphere so very much. But the best thing, of course, was having a daily satsang with MA. She would come out of Her quarters and sit quietly with a small group of devotees, talking and laughing and smiling in bright moments. I learned from the other devotees that this was a rare occurrence, and that MA was usually surrounded by a crush of people, all trying for a glimpse of Her. I felt so fortunate to have so many private audiences with Her, and to receive so many beautiful darshans during the day. When you were with MA, you never wanted to leave Her side. The vibration was so instilled with love that the bhava you would feel would just knock you over. MA would answer our questions, and She would talk to us about almost any subject of things. Oftentimes, She would tell us stories that were so funny that She was laughing hilariously, and really couldn't always complete the story. Once, She was singing a bhajan. She was singing to Krishna in a very high falsetto voice like a Hindi film star, with gestures and facial expressions, and She was dancing in a wild abhinamyam, with hand expressions. The imitation was so good that we were dying of laughter, and MA was cracking up, unable to finish the song after several attempts. She kept us all in such good humor, helping us to see the humor in life, and keeping us all light and receptive to Her incredible shakti.

At night, we would do elaborate kirtans, and MA would sing and those events were so uplifting and spiritual. MA would start singing "Hey Bhagavan," and lift right off Her vyasana, as if She was going to fly away. Several times, both Udas and I thought we saw Her levitating off the floor. She would start singing, and go into a bhava where She was singing with all Her heart and standing on Her tiptoes. Then, it seemed as if She would lift off the floor in a beam of light, and your heart would leap inside your chest. I had never felt so much bhava in my entire life. If you hung out this much with Sri Anandamayi MA, your whole life would change. I saw it happening all around me every day; such incredible miracles. Even the most hardhearted skeptics and aetheists would be broken by Her shakti. Scientists, scholars, and politicians would come and go…all of them leaving with a smile of bhakti on their faces. Even other great yogis, gurus, and sadhus would come to get some honey from the Mother Bee. MA was so happy to see them, as if She was their mother. She would care for great sadhus with such affection and love. You could see the expression in these great teachers' eyes; they loved Her so much!

photo courtesy of Shraddha

our beloved
neem karoli baba

One day, we were in the darshan hall, singing kirtana, "Govinda Jaya Jaya, Gopala Jaya Jaya…" Mother was in a quiet, ecstatic mood. Suddenly, the doors opened wide, and Neem Karoli Baba came blasting into the room, his blanket blowing to the four winds. Maharaji, as we all called him, was an incredibly high saint, and, was also the Guru of Bhagavan Das, Ram Das, Krishna Das, Hari Das Baba, and many great spiritual personalities. Mother loved him, and They would just beam at one another.

"MA, MA, the people in my ashram are being mean to me. No one understands me. They won't take care of me or feed me properly. Feed me, MA, feed me!"

Well, we all knew that his devotees adored him. They cooked the most glorious feasts for him everywhere he went, and fed him lovingly with their own hands. As a teacher, he was treated like a king.

Mother exploded with laughter. Neem Karoli Baba was such a comedian at times. They looked at one another and laughed, like two empty mirrors reflecting eternity. It was amazing to see them together. Much food was brought out to the great saint, and he had a voracious appetite. They both distributed food to all of us, and we were in awe, receiving food from the hands of such high beings! I loved it when Maharaji came to visit us. What a lion! What a Guru!

Neem Karoli Baba was so much like our father. We loved it when he came in to Vrindavan with an entourage of so many great friends like Siddhi Ma, Bhagavan Das, Ram Das, and Jai Uttal. Really, in our eyes, they were our spiritual cousins! Us devotees were always running back and forth between the two ashrams in an amazing lila. Mother loved for us to see him, and She loved to see him, too! They would smile at each other, laughing in their tremendous lilas, and when they were together, we would sing our hearts out.

❖

Maharaji looked into my eyes, and studied me pensively.

"You love Anandamyi Ma?"

"Mother, I see that he loves you very much."

I sat there, looking at him, and smiling into his wonderful eyes. He was so much fun to me; he was just so full of joy, and was a true spiritual dad. He was always moving in such an animated way, shifting back and forth, all double jointed. He would walk or support his body on his finger knuckles, just like a monkey! All of this led us to believe that he was Hanuman.

"Acha, give your lover something to eat. He looks very thin!" His head bobbed up and down. We all laughed, and he just exuded love.

Neither "Ma" nor Pa" would let us get very serious. They would act out when we got too glum. When people were slipping too deeply into a state of bhava, they always had a way of pulling us back and keeping us in the proper flow of shakti.

They both loved to feed their disciples. There was something more than food in that food. To eat the blessed food from their hands seemed to just fill your soul. I kept thinking of the people who ate the loaves that Jesus created, and how they must have felt. Food from the hands of saints seems to plant seeds that are so very magical.

Look at the marvelous people Babaji nourished: Sri Baba Hari Das, Bhagavan Das, Siddhi Ma, Ram Das, Krishna Das, Jai Uttal, and so many others. In just a short time, he changed the whole direction of spirituality in the West, and *Be Here Now* lives on, after so many years, as a Hindu Bible for westerners making the journey east.

I remember one splendid Khumba Mela, when Maharaji and Anandamayi Ma were entering the Ganges at the most auspicious moment, not far from one another, and I was somehow caught in the waters swirling between the two great saints. There was a second when I caught them both glancing over at one another; the expression on the faces of those two marvelous Gurus will be forever etched on my heart. It is undeniably the Yoga of Bliss…

❈

40

Neem Karoli Baba

the miracles of anandamayi ma

One day, it was Samyum Saptum, and it was my first experience seeing the crowds that would come when there was an advertised event with Mother. A huge tent was erected on the ashram grounds, and hundreds of people were pouring in from everywhere. Suddenly, there was a pecking order of who could see MA, or who could have darshan. They locked Her away, and I could no longer have a private darshan; also, She only came out when there were masses of people gathering in the tent. Someone told us that Prime Minister Indira Gandhi was coming to the event. Then, suddenly, there were soldiers and limousines and guards everywhere, and the whole atmosphere I had loved at the ashram was gone!

The scene in the tent was resplendent, though. MA was seated on a big white cushion, dressed in white robes, with a yellow towel on Her head. Many great gurus, swamis, and sadhus were seated on the stage with Her. The kirtan was beautiful, and so devotional. The atmosphere was very charged, with so many holy people assembled. Indira Gandhi was escorted in, wearing the only black sari and sunglasses in the crowd. She was seated in the front row, and She never even once smiled. Her demeanor was very somber and grave, like that of a woman who carried the world's woes on her shoulders. I felt bad for her having so little bhakti, or maybe it was just that she wasn't even allowed to express herself.

MA beamed, and just sort of looked over the head of Mrs. Gandhi, who received no special recognition or acknowledgement. MA treated everyone the same. Suddenly, MA announced that She wanted us all to sit quietly for a few moments in meditation. The tent became very quiet, and Mother switched on that darshan switch like only She could do. Her body became very, very bright. She so outshone any sadhu on the stage that it was staggering. There was a visibly bright white light at least four feet around Her entire body. Rays of white and gold were shooting from this light. She sat with Her hands folded in pranam and bowed to various persons. Once, I looked up at Her, and She was looking right at me, bowing and looking into my face. I felt such a rush of energy all around the top of my head, and heard and a high pitched sound, which stayed in my ears for many days. People started singing a beautiful kirtan again: "Jai MA, Jappo MA..." and Mother rose from Her cushion and left by a back exit.

I found myself walking away to a back walkway, not even knowing my own actions. It was a small back alley that I didn't even know existed. Here, from the opposite direction, came MA and Gurupriya Devi. They were sneaking down a guarded back corridor; how I found myself there, I do not know. MA seemed delighted to see me, and I fell on my face. She stopped right at my face, and I looked at Her beautiful, tiny feet. I reached forward and gently placed my hands on Her feet, which was something I had wanted to do for days. She continued to look down upon me so lovingly, and I felt a tremendous blessing passing through my body. How does one describe the electricity of what it was like to touch her? It was...otherworldly; strangely ethereal; void of material reality; hot like fire; cold like ice; sharp and soft...all of these things were running through my mind at the same time. She then gently pulled away and walked on. When I looked back at Her from where I lay on the ground, She was looking back at me. I knew that my entire life had changed in that passing glance.

The ashram was just not prepared to handle the crowds that had come to see MA. Early on in the evening, we had literally run out of food. I had gone into the village twice with Atmananda and brought back more food and supplies, and still, there was not enough. The pilgrims were hungry; some had come a long distance. Even Mrs. Gandhi was hungry, I think! What would we do? Mother was on stage, discerning the situation. She had everyone line up in a single file for prashadum. A large brass pot was brought to Her, and She blessed it. Then, She reached in, and with Her own hands, started producing prashadum for each and every person. I watched the miracle of over four hundred people receiving prashadum from a single pot. No food was in the pot originally, to my knowledge, and no one filled the pot at any time while She served everyone. Mother just kept reaching into the pot and producing prashadum for everyone. It was not a small amount, either. She even gave several people seconds! It was satisfying, delicious prashadum...I had never tasted such food at Anandamayi Ma's hand. I took my share like a

❈

43

handful of precious jewels. A devotee and I were laughing and feeling so high from eating the food MA had produced with her own hands. We kept laughing and savoring every bite. It just tasted so incredible! Finally, John, who was from England, said to me, "Jesus did it with loaves and fish…we just watched MA feed nearly five hundred people, producing the food from thin air in a single pot!" The Indians just sang kirtan louder and louder, as they were accustomed to experiencing such miracles. The Americans looked like deer caught in headlights. They were not used to witnessing miracles. I watched some young people's entire concept of reality crash that evening. Logic and reason were defied that night, and I saw a great miracle, just like something Christ would have done right before my very eyes, and manifested in the lovely, sweet form of a loving MA!

To me, the most amazing thing about Mother was how She would walk into the darshan room and look so refreshed, radiant, and dazzling, and pour out all kinds of energy as She gave inspired answers to many spiritual questions. Oftentimes, She cracked the crowd up with Her answers, as She was a great comedienne. If the atmosphere got too holy, or too profound, She would act like a child, or give the wildest answer to a question; the Indian people would laugh uncontrollably, as they understood the subtle qualities of her speech. Once, when a man asked what to do about his frequent outbursts of uncontrollable anger, Mother responded by saying he should drink a big glass of cold water, immediately! This sounded so funny in Bengali that the Bengalis screamed with laughter, and so did Mother. She was a natural cut-up, and would go from comedienne to Goddess in a heartbeat. She could control a huge crowd with a subtle glance. Then, She would launch into spiritual hymns and sing with the greatest gusto, in the soft voice of a little girl. Sometimes, She fell into huge states of bhava, and just sort of flowed with the music as She sang and sort of danced around the stage up on Her tiptoes. At these times, She was dynamic, and utterly full of energy. Then, I would see Her at the end of such a satsang, looking as though She had aged tremendously; She would be absolutely haggard, and almost near death. Attendants would help Her out of the satsang hall, moving very slowly. She would appear bent over and toothless, with a face that looked as if She had drunken all the world's poison, much like Lord Shiva, and like Him, contained it all within Her neck.

On several occasions, my feet would spontaneously rise in the satsang hall, and I would feel myself running through a corridor, as if my body was on automatic drive. And there I would be, standing, by some miraculous power, in a secret corridor where Mother was dashing away after a darshana. She always looked happy, and She would come alive when our eyes met, and there was the look on Her face of one who was greeting a long lost friend. She would call out to me as she left Samyum Saptum, "Ram, oh Ram…Ram, Ram, Ram…" She would break away as Her attendants tried to take Her away from me. She would come to where I lay in full prostration, and She would stand with Her feet near my hands. She would motion for me to rise, and when I came up on my knees, She would look into my face so kindly and sweetly as She garlanded me, saying so gently, "Serve, Ramananda, with all your heart…serve God."

Then, She would be whisked away by Her attendants, and we would part, both reaching out to another like lovers being unwillingly parted. I would wave to Her, blowing kisses her way and She would look back at me in an incredible state of bhava. Mother lived in such a Joyous Eternity.

Oh, how these meetings would make my heart sing! She just plucked at my heartstrings and made love well up in me in a way I had never experienced in my life. I could only liken it to how the gopis felt about Krishna. I loved Mother so much that I would pine for Her like a gopi. I would laugh and weep at the same time. The light and power of Her presence would make my heart flutter, and I would yearn for a touch, for a whisper, for a pranam, much like a baby seeking its mother's attention. I was lost in the ecstatic dance that is Anandamayi MA.

Surely, the Disciples must have felt this way about Jesus, Buddha, Rama, and Krishna. When you are around a pure Avatar of God, you see and feel and live in God's heaven and eternity. They carry it with them wherever they go, even though they are locked in gross physical human form. Mother looked heavenly. She walked heavenly. Everything She touched turn to gold. If She walked on a rock, we picked the rock up and kept it. If She threw away a string, we dodged for it, and kept it magnificent with her holy shakti. This is what it was like to be around a God-being.

After She rested, Mother would reappear. Now, she looked refreshed, and back into Her eternal Goddess aspect. For an older woman, She looked radiantly beautiful. She would come out smiling, and looking like the picture of health. She would speak with everyone, gesturing and being very animated. Then, She would start to laugh, and Her laugh was so infectious…your face would crack into a smile, and after awhile, She made everyone laugh. Sometimes, She told stories about devotees, and once completely cracked up as She sang a song a Hindi film star had once sung to Her! My favorite lilas were when She would tell stories about other saints, such as

Neem Karoli Baba. He could be such a jokester and cut up, thanks to that Hanuman monkey energy! We all loved Neem Karoli Baba, as, like Mother, He made us laugh, and wouldn't allow anyone to get too "religious" or serious. Mother would tell us a story, and bust up right in the middle of the story and start laughing so hard that She could not finish. Other times, there were just waves of Bliss…and laughter would come out of Her from afar…the laughter of a free spirit transmuting the Universe…the laughter of freedom…the laughter of total victory in realizing the SELF…the laughter of walking dimensionally through all maya and avidya. In Mother's case, the flame of Truth burned ever-bright with God-knowledge, Self-awareness, total psychic perception of anyone She met; She was a fountainhead of Vedic wisdom, and possessed a complete and absolute mastery over all aspects of Existence.

Can you imagine the influence on your life when you come into such intimate contact with such a Supreme Being? This is like associating with God in human form. Knowing Mother was like knowing Krishna. In such light, your heart is overwhelmed by such a presence that your mind is blown by constant Miracles, and you just surrender. There is no other path to take in the presence of such a Saint except for total and complete surrender in a state of absolute bhava and bhakti.

Mother would make a move about every four days, if not sooner. She did not tarry in one place for very long…She was always ready to GO! Life was a constant adventure, and She could constantly feel the pull of so many souls yearning for a glimpse of Her earthly form. The longest I ever saw Her stay in one place was eleven days. Most of the time, She was off in the car, heading to the train station, or heading out on a boat. Her train departures were highly publicized, and there would be an incredible crush of a crowd, everyone yearning for a glimpse of the Divine Mother.

I am not really a crowd person; yet when She made these train departures, She would insist that I come from Rishikesh to join in the satsang. I wondered why She wanted me there in those horrible train stations, in such mayhem and the crush of thousands. Then, as She looked at me and laughed, I realized intuitively that She wanted me to realize that life is like a train station. She said in Benares, "We are all waiting for the great train!" Yes, I realized that this life is like a train station. There is a train coming, and it's bound for glory! It will take us to a world much finer than this one, a heavenly world, where there is no bodily pain or grief; a beatific world full of total peace, serenity, and beauty. I watched Mother board those trains and look back, as if she were thinking, "Is anyone getting this? This train is going to Ramaloka!" I watched Her go away, looking back at me through the window, silently saying, in inward japa, "Rama, Rama, Rama, Rama, Rama…" and the train would Rama out of sight.

I laughed and pranamed, touching the floor of the dirty station, and saying, "Yes, MA, Yes MA, I got it. I got it." With each tiny, precious footstep, MA taught us. What a boon in life, to have been near such a God being.

> I saw the freedom in each footstep.
> I saw infinity in Her smile.
> She showered me with a thousand stars,
> In each loving glance.
> She lived far away, reposing within Herself.
> In Her spiritual realm, few could touch.
> Her head held in such a noble pose.
> Like an exotic Indian Maharani of tremendous beauty.
> Yet laugh a toothless, hilarious laugh
> Relaxed and free from Protocol.
> She entered Khumba Mela on an elephant's back
> With the Self Determination of Hannibal crossing the Alps!
> She danced up on Her tiptoes during satsang
> Overwhelmed with Ananda and Bhava, Ma's feet lifted from the ground
> Showing us the ultimate Bhakti, the ultimate devotee,
> Total consecrated life on the flame of Eternity!
> Oh MA, Sri Anandamayi MA, from whence shall come another Guru
> As great as Thee…whose Gaze is struck by Eternities'
> Timeless Eyes.
>
> —Swami Ramananda, Khumba Mela 1976

❊

This is all I know about the wonder, the miracle, the mystery that is Sri Sri Ananamayi MA. Each day I spent with Mother seemed like an eternity. In Her presence, all time stopped, and I found myself lost deeper and more completely in bhajans. "Jappo Ma, Jai Jai MA, OM Jappo MA Anandamayi…" There was an incredible orb of white light circling Her body. That light on many occasions seemed to take off and fly and bounce across the room, much like Glenda in "The Wizard of OZ."

I would be singing in tents with four hundred people, and just be losing myself in the bliss of kirtan. Suddenly, I would have the feeling that someone was standing right in front of me. I would open my eyes, and to my astonishment, MA would be standing right in front of me, smiling and waiting for me to open my eyes. Then, She would lift Her eyebrows and look at me much like Krishna, throw Her head back and laugh, and walk on. I would look back at Her as She left the room, and She would stop and look directly back at me, lifting Her eyebrows and grinning. My heart was so full of the pure love of prema for Her that I wanted to run after Her…"MA, MA, MA…" I could only imagine the gopis doing that sort of thing to Krishna. The energy of the lila between She and I was so similar to that energy that my heart would pine every time She left the darshan hall. My heart was so completely Hers that She kept me in continuous bhava, which seemed to always transform into mahabhava, and then into a lasting, pure, and Godly prem. When you experience this sort of thing from an Avatara, it leaves you in a permanent state of bliss.

Every lila bounces back in my mind and plays over and over, as if my being will not let go of one single experience of contact with Mother. I treasure each experience, every glance or smile She gave me, and every small flower that She handed me. I remember each little act, though so very simple, which felt so loaded with consciousness and deep spiritual meaning. During every moment I spent with Mother, She was opening my heart in such a loving way that it took me to ONENESS. All of life started flooding through my heart, until I realized that I was merged in ONENESS with everything that exists in this world, and in all worlds beyond.

After every trip I made to India to see Mother, I came back to America more and more transformed. When I would get back to California, I would see visibly how much I had changed, just by people's reactions to me. I felt inwardly lighter and lighter, as if the cesspool of my thoughts, experiences and body were being eaten. When the karma starts to disappear in the presence of a

Sat Guru, you suddenly become more of the spirit, and much less of this physical world. I noticed that many of my friends who were with Mother a lot would start to add a lot of weight. This occurred in order for them to stay grounded in this world. We felt so light in Her presence, and some felt very uncomfortable being a spirit in a physical world! I personally loved it! So, I kept getting thinner, more supple, and kept attaining more of an ancient yogic body. As far as I can tell, I got a whole new physical body after my first darshan with MA. The disease-ridden, weak body of my childhood was gone, and I got a new body that looked like Hanuman! I saw many of my childhood friends during this period, and they did not even recognize me. Many exclaimed, "You got a new body!" It was then that I realized that MA had turned me into a little version of the monkey god! No wonder, then, that in my heart, I just treasured the feeling of heading back to the Nanital, and being with Sri Nccm Karoli Baba!

I think MA gave me a new body so that I could handle India...so that I could go back and forth between America and India to see Her; trek through the Himalayas; sleep on temple floors; eat very simply; and stay well. Wow! I was no longer a wimp! JAI MA!

photo courtesy of Swami Ramananda

Swamiji's Reappearance

Mother would move every four days, on the average. She was on a regimen of travel, and it seemed to just keep spreading the shakti. Being an Aquarian, I loved that lifestyle, and so I always had the shakti to go with Her, wherever I was invited to go. We would leave Deradune in caravan and head for Benares, but there would be wonderful little stops along the way, at places like Nama Shiranya and Kanpur. Mother had delightful little ashrams and roadside shrines in all of those areas. Nama Shiranaya is really a special spot; it is where Sita used to live, in her final exile from Ram, with their two sons. I could feel just how special the energy was there. Mother would just completely relax there, and could be so candid with just a few devotees in such a small spot. We loved such visits, because we knew we could spend a lot of darshan time with Her.

I was such a greedy bhakta, just sitting with Her in that little cabin, caressed by jasmine winds. The vibration was so high, so electric…I was constantly filled with bliss in Her presence. The conversation would be high-minded, and yet casual. Mother would tell very funny stories, and the Bengali women would go from states of hilarious laughter to falling into trance-like states, where they sat there so quietly in Her presence, like gently swaying sphinxes.

Mother wanted me to accompany her on to Benares, and I was a bit reticent. That was where my dear Swami Shankarananda had gone on to leave his body; I did not really want to face that, and I was hanging onto my happiness. However, it was more opportunity for instruction from Her lips, and it was Her appearance day lila, which was considerably significant. On Mother's birthday, She would go quite out of Her body in a huge samadhi as the devotees sang so sweetly to Her, as though She was a sleeping child. She would look like sleeping beauty in a wonderful white pandal, covered with gorgeous flower garlands, flowers and incense; Her face would turn very pale, and would look almost as though She were in maha samadhi. After awhile, the devotees would place Her on a huge, throne-like Palaquin, and carry Her through the ashram in this deep state of nirvana. She would look absolutely lifeless. Songs would raise so high in bhajans, and She would return to Her divine source for a day or so, leaving Her lifeless body for us to tend to! It was scary to see Her look so completely absent from her body!

She explained to Didi Ma that the Gods were feeding Her on the other side during this time, and that Her auspicious appearance day was Her chance to visit with them. It was a remarkable experience to witness.

In the midst of all the crush of crowds, and MA looking so lifeless, I felt a warm hand on my shoulder. I turned around, and nearly jumped out of my skin. It was my beloved Swami Shankaranandaji! I started to weep in his arms.

"Swamiji I can't believe you are alive! Is this you, or is this an apparition?"

"Ramananda my son, it is I."

My eyes studied his face. He looked so strong and beautiful.

"Swamiji, was it not your time?"

"I walked here to Benares. I actually stopped eating on the way, and was only taking water as I anticipated Maha Samadhi. But this did not happen. No matter how much I fasted, I did not leave my body. Then, I had a dream, and Mother came to me and said that I was not to leave at that time. She told me I was your teacher, and told me to not abandon such a young student who needed me. She spoke to me directly, and the dream was very real."

"Oh Swamiji, Mother is so merciful. I have missed you so much. I just couldn't believe you would leave me…"

"But you see, by my leaving, you met your Guru. I knew I must go to make room in your heart for Her. So everything is perfect, and this is all Her lila." He was laughing, hugging me and patting me on the back.

"Shiva is truly a great God, to give me both of you!"

Swamiji and I have remained friends to this day, and I have made many journeys back to India to be with him. This year marks thirty-three years of our friendship, and when we are in India together, we continue to visit ashrams and holy places, and meet with great teachers, yogis, and gurus. What a blessing Swami Shankaranandaji is in my life; I am so glad it was *not* his time!

ma ma ma jai jai ma ma ma ma jai jai ma!

When Mother came out of Her trance, we celebrated with a huge meal. She was placing Her shakti in the food. We ate with gusto; that food She blessed was the best-tasting food in the world! It tasted like it was full of seeds of bhakti. She was putting Her spirit inside of us. She always told us to carry this shakti to all the people who could not come to India to be directly with Her.

"They will feel me in your hugs and well wishes, and they will see me in your smile."

We became quite concerned, because Mother had stopped eating at this time. She had gone several weeks without any food or water. I was around Her constantly, and She never wavered in Her lack of desire for food. The attendants around Mother were getting concerned, and were uneasy that She would go into Mahasamadhi if She didn't eat. I was never concerned, because I could see Her feeding each day on the sunlight. She was doing these amazing kriyas as She looked up at the sun, and each time, Her body would start to glow. Food seemed so mundane to such a being! Finally, She said to us, "My food is dedicated lives."

Sri Sri Anandamayi MA is much more than my Guru. She is my friend. When She asked me to return to Southern California to teach yoga and be a Swami, I wanted just to stay by Her side forever. The moment I had that thought, She looked directly into my eyes in a private darshan, and said, "You can separate matter from matter, but never spirit from spirit. In spirit, we are always one."

Those were Her last words to me. She asked me to carry Her shakti to "all of Her children who cannot come to India," and that all I really had to do was walk the energy and stay mindful of Her; She would do the rest.

I can say that this has been absolutely true. I have been in bliss now for thirty years. I have never known a dark moment when MA wasn't absolutely surrounding me with her love. Even during my rave and club periods in Los Angeles and New York City, I felt Her dancing right alongside of me! I would look up in the rafters of the discos, and I could see Her sitting there, smiling down at me! I have never, felt alone. Her feet have seemed so firmly planted in my heart. Mother told me, "I will never leave you...and once someone has seen me, they will never forget me." How true...how very true.

What does it feel like to live every day in the shakti of such a great teacher; an avatara who is a perfect, angelic saint? There is no drug on this planet that can make a person feel the high I feel at every moment. Even in my dreams, I sit with Her, and they feed me on the other side. Mother cares for me completely. Each day feels like a poem, and is just so blessed. I am a very happy man. Even just taking a walk is an ecstatic experience for me. I hear the flowers singing, and I watch them changing colors. Birds light on my head like they did for St. Francis! I walk each day here in Rancho Mirage on the mountainside behind my house; the Bighorn sheep walk alongside me, and kittens follow me down the path. The whole world is now my home, and all the people, animals, and trees are my family. They are my brothers and sisters, my cousins, my uncles and aunts, and my mothers and daughters.

All the animals seem so very sweet; they are so simple and caring in their own way. All the trees and flowers, rocks and stones, insects, and birds of the sky...everything is swirling in Oneness.

My friends, I can honestly say to you...there is only LOVE.

I love each and every one of you who are reading this book. I want to reach out and touch each one of you; I want to hold you and hug you and wipe away your tears. I want to touch your feet and call you my teacher. Don't you see the incredible miracle of LIFE? We are all totally interconnected, a woven part of one another. In that innermost essence of being, there is just LOVE. All illusions and fears fall away; all ego and selfishness disappear; all desires seem to just blow away in the wind; and all that is left is the presence of the Eternal ONE.

With the JOY of this knowledge and the blessing of my dear guru Sri Anandamayi MA, can we not all just embrace in an enormous world wide group hug? I feel Mother calling to us all:

"My children, share this beautiful world in Peace. Love one another. Share what you have together. Make the Earth a beautiful garden, and know that I love each one of you."

"You are the Sunlit children of a golden dawn." —Sri Aurobindo

"TRANSFORM…" —the Mother of Sri Aurobindo Ashram said.

"SOAR…" —Baba Muktananda said to me.

"There is only LOVE. .!" —cried Neem Karoli Baba

"YOU ARE ALL BLESSED SOULS…" —Sri Nirmalananda Swami sings to us.

"I am ever with each one of you, wherever you happen to be; but your vision is tied down to worldly matters, and you have little time to direct your eyes to this body in all your thoughts and actions. What can I do? Know for certain that whatever you do in thought and deed, whether you are near or in distant lands, never escapes my attention…just as at the flash of torchlight your faces gleam forth in their bold outlines, all your facial expressions appear in my mind when you meditate on me or talk about me or sit down to pray for me."

—Sri Sri Anandamayi MA

I have enjoyed so many glorious trips back to India, and so many lilas with my beloved Swami and my Beloved MA. There were joyous times, too many to enumerate, on the bhakti train of Mother's many journeys. Now, they all blend into a beautiful bubble of bliss as She showers Her love constantly upon all of us. Mother took Her Mahasamadhi on August 27th, 1982, at the wonderful age of eighty-seven years.

However, She has not gone anywhere. She told us that She was the same during life as She was before birth, and that, "though the years march through the hall of eternity," She always remained the same. Even now, I tell you, She is VERY active. Now, there is no body to limit Her love, and She is traveling, traveling everywhere, with no limitations. Answer that knock at your heart's door! She is standing there, waiting for you to open up. Let Her into your heart, and discover your Divine Self.

I LOVE YOU…JAI MA!
Swami Ramananda

ma

bhakti
rasa
darshan

jai ma jai ma
sri ma om ma
jai ma!

All poems by Swami Ramananda

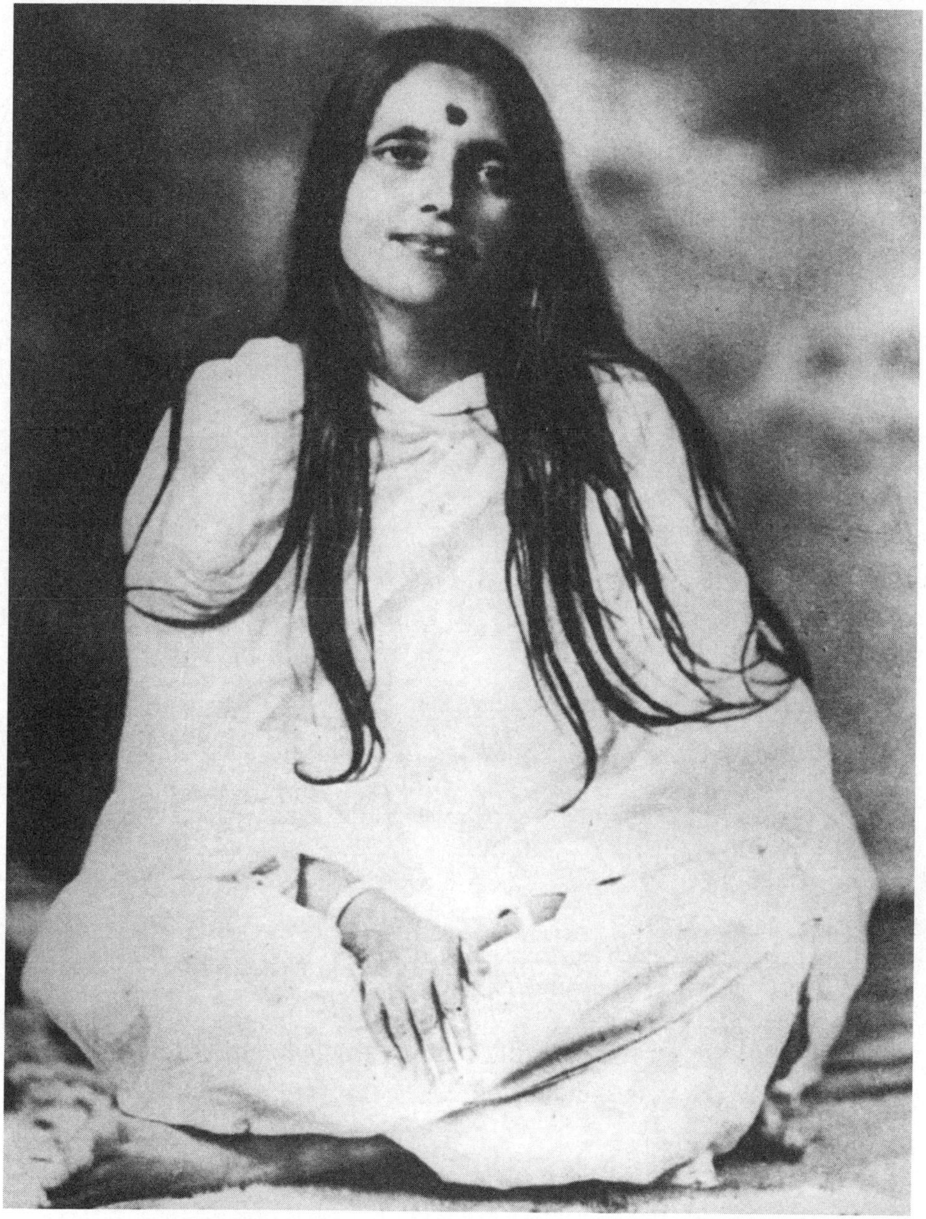

What joy!
     What laughter!
          Bliss beyond words!
               Oh dearest Mother, you taught us to Laugh
                   at life's seeming ups and downs…
     You keep us on the path to Happiness!
     How could we ever believe the illusion of this maya
       and allow it to bring our souls so low?

Help us see all the positive things you pointed out about life.
     Let us not stray from your teaching
        To be Simple,
           Non attached to the material world,
              Non defined by material things,
                To find the Joy in our
                   Inner Treasures…
When I think of your smile, your loving touch,
        your gentle words, and heartfelt bhajans-
        I cannot get caught up in this world,
        I live in your blissful world.

Let us strike out searching for that Path of Joy…
     Let us walk the path of perfect Peace,
       May our lives not be wasted chasing maya!
       May our Joy be Infinite with Thee!

                            —Vrindavan, 1981

❖

photo courtesy of Matri Sangha

Walking the Himalayas alone,
The wind caresses my face
As I look at the far off snow wall of Tibet,
An ancient voice is singing to me
And I realize that you are here, dear God.

Awaken in me the Sunlight of my Soul,
Pick me up from this dusty road
Clean me off Lord, wash away the karmic stains
Set me upright again
Let me smile a True Smile
Let your Light embrace my Soul!

I lift my eyes to the Hills
Where the mighty Ganges sings,
And the glory of your creation
Overwhelms me with Nature's ancient beauty
All I see around me exists within
The greatest temple is within the Human Heart.

Oh Lord, help us find that Truth,
Lead us on the Sylvan Path
Open our diamond-crusted hearts
And let us sing a thousand songs of Joy
Sitting in the inner Cave of Truth
There is Eternal Peace.

Standing in the icy Ganges snow melted waters
Ma Ganga splashing running over my face
You've washed your child anew
Oh great and wonderful Soul of all Existence!

—Mt. Kailasha, 2001

60

Oh, Mother of bliss. . .

❈

Oh Mother of bliss…

my heart is melting for you…

you touched my

heart

and made it

Sing!

Mystic MA

Amidst the nerve-jangling traffic, the crush of humanity, cries and woes vampirizing the Night of our Consciousness; the wicked dance of mayas deception, the political half truths, Betrayed friendships…Insanity of fake promises and Dissolution of morality, ethics and Anything Kind. Beyond the Avidya, the Maya, the INSANITY…
I hear that Mystic Call

> On etheric Wings
> So full of Light,
> Elusive and Pure,
> Eternal Mantram,
> Ineffable,"OM MA"
> She is the Peace that passeth Understanding.
> Her name is written on the Clouds.
> Her Loka is my Happy Place.
> She is Home.

How wonderful is your healing touch…
Oh Joy
Oh bliss
incarnate…

You shine like the noonday
SUN…

Mother, every time I look at you, I feel tears falling from eyes…but they are not tears of sorrow…they are tears of transformation. I feel you changing me from the inside out…

All that I am, and All that I have, is yours…

❈

The minute I prayed that prayer, I realized that I am the richest man in the world!

Once you give God everything, you merge in Oneness with all things.

Open my eyes, that I may see, visions of Love, Thou hast for me…Open my eyes, illumine me…Spirit Divine!

—Christian hymn

❖

JAI MA

That Her precious white wrapped body touched this Earth, softly walking on Angelic feet—
Is a blessing mankind can only wait for Ages hoping to See…Her cascading laughter rushing over the Rocks and Obstacles of our Minds, cleansing our Soul like the Mighty Ganga itself…Her bliss Soaring up through the Clouds like the courageous flight of Garuda unbound…Alone, replendent, MA sits and smiles like the Ageless Kailasha, Unsoiled, Fountainhead of Wisdom, Love Incarnate, Bliss Everlasting…That we should be so Blessed, To be touched by such a gaze of Perfect Love.

  When all else fails to move us,
    In our stubborn Sleep.
     And even when our Hearts are hardened…
      Those mystic words of MA break through every Rigid Night,
      Any hateful negative thought dispelled by Her lingering gaze,
        Angelic Face, and Sunlit Presence.

OM MA, SRI MA

You said you would never leave us that we would be Yours
Forevermore; Unbroken Golden Cord of Shakti, O Holy One,
You Alone are Truth
And give these Restless Souls a Home.

—Swami Ramanada
2.20.2000

❈

Mother of Joy, Mother of Peace,
Take my heart and make it yours. Know
you are the sunlit path and joy incarnate…

Pitaji, MA, Paramahansa Yogananda

Jai
MA!

You touched my heart, and made it sing

Sri Anandamayi Ma Mahasamadhi

1895-1982

August 27, 1982

Age 87 years young

❖

Oh Joyous friend, guruji
Oh playmate incarnate OM MA
Mother your eyes dance like diamonds
Your aura shines like the noonday Sun.
Your Spirit makes me smile
You bring out the best part of all of us.
Who could have such mercy
to bring me to your embrace?
Is this reality? I am pinching myself?
With each glance I am transported
to Rama Loka.
What heavenly world are we living in
here in Deradune?
You are blinding me with your Light
Everywhere is holiness and purity
You are the incarnation of Love
I have never seen such love as your love.
Angels seem to fly all around your halo.
I realize time is standing still
At your holy touch, I have tasted
Immortality.

—Rajport Himalayas 1974

In India, we respect all women as living manifestations of the Goddess…

photo courtesy of Bhakti Rasa

…Especially older women, our Mothers, who brought the miracle of your life to this planet, are worthy of great respect.

❀

PRAY:

Oh Mother, I humbly bow and take refuge at your Lotus Feet. Teach me, lead me, nourish me in the Truth. Then and only then may I find peace and happiness…

photo by Saraswati

JAI MA to all my MAs!

❁

Jai Mother Paravati!

❁

Jai Lakshmi!

❁

Jai Durga!

❁

Jai Kali MA!

❁

Jai Sita MA!

❁

Jai MA Radharani!

❁

Jai Ma Saraswati!

❁

pathways to bliss!

yogic lifestyle

bhakti yoga (Love)

diet
(You Are What You Eat!)

japa yoga (Mantra)

creating an ashram
(Spiritual Community)

hatha yoga
(Exercise)

personal relationship
(with a Guru)

...ace...)

meditation

satsang
(Hanging with Saints)

karma yoga
(Selfless Service)

sense of humor
(A Must For Survival)

Lord Chaitanya Mahaprabhu

bhakti yoga

"You only need love; you don't need a practice."
—Tat Wala Baba of Rishikesh, Himalayas

Bhakti Yoga is the yoga of love and devotion. In India, this manifests as your daily practice of expressing your devotion to God, by caring for your deities; by offering worship with lamps, bells, water, flowers, fruits; and by singing bhajans, or hymns, to your gods and gurus. In a Hindu home, one rises early in order to bathe properly, dress their best, and then tend to their deities, which, in a Bhakti home, are bathed, oiled, perfumed and dressed daily. Then, the deities are fed, and they receive worship. All the food prepared in your home should first be offered to your deities. That makes it consecrated food and holy prashadum.

"If you eat only Holy prashadum and consecrated food, your life will be blessed beyond measure. All health problems will fall away, and you will live a long and healthy life. The rule here is to always remember God first. Awaken every morning to tend to your deities; make offerings of fruits and flowers; sing praises to God; and offer your food to God and Guru before partaking…these acts will bless your life beyond measure. This is the beginning of Bhakti, and will lead you into the Heart of Love."

—Swami Shankarananda Giri

In the Himalayas, Swami Shankarananda and I traveled often to Gangotri to the ashram there near the source of the Ganges. This ashram is completely based on the Bhakti Yoga lifestyle. We awoke each morning at 4:00 a.m. and took a cold plunge in the Ganges. Then, we dressed in our finest clothes, with a warm chowdar. At that high elevation, mornings were always cold. The crispness of the air invaded our bodies during pranayama techniques, and there was a wonderful Himalayan purity everywhere.

Imagine this: you stand at the doorway of the Shiva Temple, reciting your mantras, or doing Japa Yoga. Suddenly, the doors burst open, and there, you start your day by seeing Shiva shining and magnificently dressed in beautiful dhotis. Shiva is covered with flowers; bells ring, conches are being sounded, the lamps of many flames are being waved, and everyone is singing the Shiva Chalisa.

You watch this spectacle every morning, day after day, week after week, with the roar of the Ganges by the side of the temple; your heart just fills with bliss!

Then, you go to the Krishna Temple and see the beautiful deities…washed and oiled and painted so beautifully. Sometimes, in India, all of the clothes the deities wear are made of flowers. They stand there, shining in their finest jewelry, smiling, and dancing and bestowing love and compassion. This is the spirit of the God dancing in your life.

You have offered your very best at the Lotus Feet of God and Guru. This wonderful practice of devotion through worship will take you deeply into bliss.

In India, Swamiji and I just wandered from temple to temple. I had the darshan of so many deities between temples, from the Himalayas to Benares, to Haridwar, to Vrindavan, and on to the magnificent temples of South India. I became so full of that light, and LOVE for God, that I would merge into my higher vibration.

Devotion transforms the face. It takes us out of our selfishness and ignorance, and throws our hearts directly into bliss. When we get our little egos out of the way, the full light of God's love can shine in our hearts. This is the purpose of Bhakti. You love God so much that everything in your life gets purified.

"In the Kali Yuga, Bhakti Yoga is the easiest and fastest way to enlightenment."

—Swami Shankarananda Giri

When you are first starting out, of course, you cannot have as spectacular a home altar as the ones in these magnificent temples. But you can make it very nice in your way. Just pick out one deity that you truly love, and a teacher who you truly love and respect. Start out with a photo or a small deity, and find a special place in your home where you can worship them. This is the start of a Bhakti practice.

Then, slowly start putting your energy into making that place more special. Give the deity clothes…especially if it is Krishna; this is a huge blessing for your home. Place water there daily. Give that spot flowers and fruits. Burn incense there constantly. Anytime you feel love for God in your heart, offer some incense and take a moment and pray there.

"We can at least give God fifteen minutes a day. He gives us a whole twenty-four hours. If you spend fifteen minutes a day in silent meditation and worship, you will start on the path that leads to purification and peace."

—Sri Anandamayi MA

How to Create an Altar

Your home is your temple. It is critical, for yogic practice, to have that special place in your home where you worship or meditate. It is that sacred spot where you place a candle, a deity, a picture of your teacher, burn incense, and offer flowers. This will build a spiritual atmosphere in your home, and will keep you focused on yoga.

First, take a compass, and find out the directional layout of your home or living space. In Hinduism, the Vastu Vidya Shastras are scriptures pertaining to how to make your home into a temple. Since every Hindu home is a temple, it's important to pay attention to these directives for the placement of bedrooms, altars, kitchens, fireplaces, and baths. This will bring good vastus, good living, and good rest into your life.

According to the Vastu Vidya Shastras, the best wall for an altar is a west-facing wall. Try to clear a space. According to the Vastus, the best colors for a meditation wall are blue or green, which seem to create an atmosphere of peace. In India, oftentimes a person will cover that wall in a beautiful blue or green sari. You can do this quite simply with a staple gun.

Then, find a nice altar table. If you plan to sit on the floor, it can be low. It doesn't have to be the world's greatest table. You can always drape it with a sari or a chowdar.

Next, decide on your central deities. There are three million Hindu gods and goddesses to pick from. Also, Hindus will accept worship in any other tradition. They really are that open-minded. I once saw a woman in South India place the pictures of Mahatma Ghandi, Martin Luther King, Jesus, Sai Baba, and the Jackson Five on her altar table, and offer fire arati and incense to all of them as her gurus. Hinduism is really that disorganized and synthetic. Your guru can be anyone who teaches or inspires you. We offer respect to those persons through arati.

In creating your altar, place your main deity, or Ishta, in the very center. If you like Radha Krishna deities, it is good to bathe and oil them daily, and to place fresh clothing on them. It brings a huge purification into the home. It is not so critical to dress Lord Shiva, because he is a sadhu, and usually wears only a tiger skin. Your deities can have crowns and jewelry, as your budget permits. The more opulent, the better. Also, Krishna will need a flute, Shiva needs a trident, and Subramanium needs a spear. If you have a lot of deities, you can rotate them to the central position. Take a look at your altar, and try to keep it clean, simple, and beautiful.

❖

You will need some small cups of water for your deities, as drinking water should be offered to them daily. Also, you will need small plates for prashadum. You need these following items to perform a good puja:

❖ large brass or silver plate

❖ arati lamp

❖ camphor fire tablets

❖ water container and spoon: these usually come in a set, and are brass (optional)

❖ chowry (yak tail fly whisk)

❖

- ❖ peacock feather fan
- ❖ bell (usually has vehicle of Ishta on the top or Ganesha)
- ❖ conch (shell horn)
- ❖ small brass or silver plates for offered food
- ❖ incense and incense holder
- ❖ vibhuti and kumkum
- ❖ flower holders, fruits, and money

Performing Puja

The bell is rung throughout the entire puja. First, offer incense to Lord Ganesha, saying, "OM Nama Ganapati Namaha." Then, offer incense, fire, conch, flowers, sweets and fruits to all of your other deities. If you have a lingam, you should place drops of water on the lingam, and repeat, "Om Nama Shivaya." If you have deities of Krishna, you should use the chowri and peacock fans to fan the deities as you ring the bell and chant, "Hare Krishna, Hare Krishna, Krishna Krishna, Hare Hare, Hare Rama, Hare Rama, Rama Rama, Hare Hare." Finally, perform all the same things to Mother, as your Guru. Offer MA the flame, conch, flowers, and water in a small glass by Her picture, sweets and fruits. Then, using the peacock fan, chant over and over again, "Jai Ma, Jai Ma, Jai Ma…"

Then, follow this experience with five minutes of silent meditation. You should do at least fifteen minutes of silent meditation daily. Mother says that we owe God at least fifteen minutes of silence a day. It's not much to ask. I offer at least three, five-minute meditations daily after puja, at 5:00 a.m., noon, and 6:00 p.m. The gods should all be fed at that time in a small dish, and should be offered whatever food you have to eat first. That makes everything you eat mahaprashadum, and consecrated with their shakti…

❖

photo by Saraswati

Pilgrimage to a Hindu Temple

One of the most beautiful things about the time period we live in is that India has come to the West. There are now fifty-four Hindu temples in the Los Angeles area alone. There are beautiful Hindu temples throughout the United States, and myriad yoga ashrams. What a blessing it is to be able to have this atmosphere, and not even have to face the many hours of flying time to India. Paramahansa Yogananda said that one day, Los Angeles would become the Benares of the West. What insightful words, as nearly any food, cultural event, and South and North Indian-

photo courtesy BBT, International Society for Krishna Consciousness

style temples can be found in L.A. today. The city of Artesia, or "Little India," along with the resplendent Hindu Temple in the mountains above the ocean in Malibu, are witnesses to Paramahansaji's words.

The general public of any faith is welcome in a Hindu Temple. You must, however, observe the following rules, out of respect. First, always bathe beautifully before a temple experience, and wear clothing that fully covers the body, preferably a sari or khourta. Second, bring something to offer God, such as fruits, sweets, incense, flowers, or money. Always leave your shoes outside the temple compound, observe silence inside the sanctuaries, and watch the Indian people. Try to follow just what they are doing, in order to show respect in a holy place of worship. Really watch what you say inside a temple; the Gods and Goddesses are all listening.

Why would you go to a Hindu temple? You can go for prayer or meditation; for spiritual help; to celebrate birthdays, weddings, memorial services, yagnas for dedications of spiritual names, and Hindu festivals; and to consult a priest. Seeing the beautiful Hindu Gods, who are always smiling and so happy to see you, is a wonderful experience

Make your offering, ring the temple bell, bow down to your deities, and circumambulate the temple for a blessing. Every sincere prayer is answered. Your true, pure devotion will grant you a boon. A visit will give you bliss.

One day, my dear friend, Swamini Turiyasangitananda, Alice Coltrane, told me she was trying to procure some land on which to build a lovely ashram for her yoga students and devotees. I told her that we must first perform a Ganesha puja at the newly-built Ganesh temple in Malibu. So, I prepared a lovely offering of fruits, sweets, incense, and coconuts, all arranged on pure silver trays. We went to the temple together, met with the priests, and prayed for the land. I gave Ganesha everything, and even left the trays there with a sum of money or Lakshmi, given as a dakshina to the Great God.

Swamini and I circumambulated the temple together, and stood in front of the Lord, holding hands. I was so happy to share this blessed moment with such a divine being. I love the wonderful music that Alice Coltrane has offered to the world, and I would do anything to be of help to her ministry. We left, carrying beautiful roses that the temple priest had given us, and a smiling peace came into our hearts. A few days later, Swamini was given the land near Malibu for an ashram. The prayers had been answered, and it had been a beautiful, blessed visit to Lord Ganesha.

"To Ramananda: There is no doubt that you shall take Liberation in this very lifetime. May the Lord guide you onward to the divine goal."

—OM Turiyasangitananda (Alice Coltrane)

Daily Observances

Morning Pranayam

You should practice morning pranayam the first thing you do when you wake up. Don't reach for that coffee or turn on the news…first, bathe; then light a candle, and sit quietly while you open your breathing program. Assume Vishnu mudra by dropping your index finger and third finger of your right hand, and placing your thumb against your right nostril and your fourth finger against your left nostril. This technique is called Nadishodhana pranayama.

Now, inhale through the right nostril by removing the thumb, and hold for five counts. Circulate the air in the nasal lock. Then, exhale by lifting your finger and expelling through your left nostril. Then, lock and hold five counts with no air in the lung chamber. Then, inhale through the left, and hold; then expel through the right. Do this back and forth at least seven times. It brings balance and quiet to the nerves, and also opens the nasal passages.

The most important yogic breathing technique is Ujjayi, or Victorious Breath. If you use this technique properly, you can gain control of the prana. Draw the air in through your nostrils by contracting the glottis in the back of your throat. This is a long draw of air, and the inner sound is much like the ebb and flow of the ocean surf. The exhalation is twice as long as the inhalation. Listen to the inner sound as air passes over the flattened glottis and creates the surf like sound. This practice will relax you deeply, and you will watch your shoulders drop and your whole body come to peace as you practice this pranayam inwardly. It will prepare you for meditation.

Meditation

The breathing technique will pull you right in. If possible, sit on the floor in Padmasana, which pulls both ankles locking and feet above knees. If you cannot do this, try to sit in Sukhasana, or easy posture. Lift up your spine straight, as if there is a plumb line passing through the top of your head, and directly align down the back and buttocks. Sit up! Keep up the deep Ujjayi breathing.

Focus your mind on one thing if you want to see the oneness in all things. Allow your mind to call a visualization of a still lotus resting on a large blue lake reflecting the moonlight. Do not let your mind stray from this vision…breathe it into your soul. On each inhalation and exhalation, inwardly say, "OM NAMAH SHIVAYA." Then, each breath is an offering to Lord Shiva, and He will grant you the boon of inner peace. At the end of your meditation, bow your head.

There are a lot of great guided meditation tapes out there. I think they are great for beginners, and help keep your mind from sabotaging your meditation.

Sometimes it is easier to quiet down by listening to someone with a great, hypnotic voice. However, it is equally important to spend time in silence. When you master true silence, you will delve much deeper within your meditation. You will have a rich, radiant experience of your inner being, and you may also hear the nadis, or inner sounds, as well. They chime sometimes, almost like bells. This opens all the chakras, and will take you right to your God Self.

"Set to work while there is yet time, and try to kindle the inner light. In the hearth of the mind, ignite the fire of Self-inquiry, or the fire of God's name. Fan it into a blazing flame by association with the Holy and Wise, and by prayer and meditation. Little by little, this light will grow bright and steady, and will illumine you both inwardly and outwardly; thereby, the path to Self realization will be made easy."

—Sri Anandamayi MA

"I built a tower here on the side of the mountain, where I can climb up and sit quietly, undisturbed, day or night. In the daytime, I sit there and watch the sun rise and set in myriad beautiful colors. The sky is like a vast painting of pink, orange, azure, and turquoise. At night, I sit there quietly, and the moon rises and sets. The Milky Way galaxy is resplendent over my head, like a river of shimmering diamonds. As I sit there quietly, day and night, such waves of BLISS pass through my body, and I am transformed into my GOD SELF. My friends, you must develop a meditation practice to find Bliss. You must go there every opportunity, day or night, and sit quietly. Find your special spot for Sadhana; this is half of the battle. Go there religiously, and meditate. Empty your mind of needless thoughts, and the peace will descend. Bliss will explode in your consciousness like fireworks. God does everything for us; we only have to let go and SIT."

—Swami Ramananda

Japa Yoga

Japa is the repetition of God's name or mantra (sacred words), which can lead you to bliss. These names, or mantras, are usually counted on a mala (or prayer beads, which consists of one hundred eight beads. There are mystical reasons for this number, and it is prescribed in the scriptures that one round consists of one hundred eight repetitions.

> "The more you repeat God's name, the more you will soar into bliss. The name on your lips of Rama or Shiva or Krishna or MA will taste like nectar. With each round of bead counting you are reversing all negative karmas, you are cleansing the mind. The more you focus on God, the more you will find Bliss. Do Japa!"

> —Swami Shankarananda Giri

The technique for Japa Yoga is simple. Always count the beads using your right hand. At the Hare Krishna Temples, they sell wonderful bead bags which protect your beads. These bags have a hole for the index finger. You should not use the index or second finger when counting or fingering beads. This is the finger used in accusation, and it is, shall we say, an unholy finger. Treat your beads as God. They are receiving God's name. Otherwise, you will not get the positive effects of doing japa.

"Swamiji, when should I practice Japa?"

You can do Japa at all times. This is a really good practice to do in the car when you are stuck in traffic. It will keep your mind peaceful. Count beads when you are doing housework or chores. Count beads when you wake up, and count beads before you sleep. Keep the mantra running all day long. All of the saints and holy persons I have spent time with were constantly performing Japa, and this is what kept them in bliss, and connected.

> "You should try to perform 15,000 rounds of Japa mantra weekly."

> —Sri Anandamayi MA

> "150,000 crores (150,00 million repeats) of Lord Rama's name, and you will take liberation."
> —Swami Sivananda

photo of A.C. Bhaktivedanta Swami Prabhupada, courtesy of the BBT, ISKCON

"I am chanting 'HARE KRISHNA' with every inhalation and exhalation, even in my sleep. This is why I am in bliss. This is the source of my happiness… God's name." —Swami Shankarananda Giri

Here are some simple mantras for Japa Yoga. Remember one per bead. When you reach the guru bead(the bead with the tuft of thread on it), reverse and go back the opposite direction.

- OM RAMA (ending "a" is silent; pronounced, "Rahm")
- OM MA

- OM NAMAH SHIVAYA (Ohm Nahma Sheevahya)
- JAI MA (victory to Mother)
- SITA RAM
- HARE KRISHNA, HARE KRISHNA, KRISHNA KRISHNA, HARE HARE, HARE RAMA, HARE RAMA, RAMA RAMA, HARE HARE
- OM GOD
- OM JESUS

You can take the name of any god, goddess, or guru that appeals to you, as well. During the repetition of the name, try to mentally identify more and more with your Ishta Devata (your primary God). With each bead, cry out your love and devotion. IT WORKS!

"I was searching for Swami Ramananda on the mountainside where he lives, to tell him there was a huge fire burning nearby. I was worried about him. I found him up on the mountainside, quietly meditating on a large rock. He was a vision of peace, and it was obvious that he was gone far away from his body. I gently cleared my throat and pranamed. Swamiji opened his eyes, and looked at me directly. I told him there was a huge forest fire burning nearby. Firemen had tried to put it out for several hours, to no avail. He stood up on the rock, lifted his hands into the beautiful blue sky, and started loudly chanting, "JAI MA, SRI MA, OM MA, JAI MA…" It seemed like his whole body was shaking. Suddenly, from what seemed to be blue skies, there was a torrential rain. It was such a downpour! I ran back to the ashram. Swamiji sat back down on the rock, and went back into his meditations. The fire was extinguished.He showed me that day the power of japa and mantra and faith."

—Rukmini Devi

Hatha Yoga

Hatha Yoga is your daily practice of yoga postures. By combining techniques of stretching and breathing with your Bhakti and devotion, you can enter into bliss. A lot of people think Hatha is the only yoga, and the fad of yoga classes in gyms across America seems pretty devoid of devotion to me. It is time to put God back into the center of our yoga practice, and Hatha Yoga is by no means an end in itself. There are a lot of very sullen, unhappy yogis out there who are going through a lot of pain, and not getting very far in their sadhana, to prove this fact.

These postures often times with different animal names like "the cat," "the lion," and "the fish"…are aimed at stretching your body and detoxifying your body. This, combined with proper breathing techniques, is what will bring the bliss. You want to look forward every day to these wonderful stretches, and to dedicate every move you do to finding God. Long ago, the rishis designed these postures to bring enlightenment and bliss into the body, so they need to be performed with the same reverence and devotion that one does in Japa, or in any other spiritual practice.

Sri Anandamayi MA instructed me to study yoga with my teacher in Rishikesh. The atmosphere there in the foothills of the Himalayas was perfect for yoga practice. We awoke every day and took our plunge in the Ganges, and then studied yoga on a rock ledge above the rocky rapids. Learning Sarvangasana in that atmosphere, with the air tinged with Himalayan jasmine, was fantastic. I highly recommend this, if your life ever allows this opportunity. Study Hatha in India.

Asana Practice

Try this as a daily regiment:

- Hero Series(these are the postures taught by Lord Rama to his troops)
- Suryanamaskar (sun salutation series)
- Aparnasana (nose to knee position, important for detoxification)
- Sarvangasana (shoulder stand)
- Halasana (plow)
- Sasangasana (rabbit pose)

- ∞ Agnisara (inner fire)
- ∞ Matsyasana (the fish)
- ∞ Bhujapidasana (the crow)
- ∞ Banarasana (monkey posture)
- ∞ Shirshansana (the headstand)
- ∞ End with Natarajasana (the king pose)

This will give you a great stretch before work. You will chant God's name all day long if you live like this. It will be a great great blessing to your life.

Here are pictures and descriptions of each of the poses. Remember: in yoga, there is nothing and no one to compete with. Go at your own ability, and steadily stretch your muscles until you can spend more time in each pose, and with a great flexibility. Don't force your body into poses, or you can injure yourself. Instead, gently learn them and integrate them into your body language. There is no reason to rush; you have all of eternity to learn to be a yogi.

all yoga posture photos by Saraswati

A great way to start your day…be a HERO!

These were the series of postures taught by Lord Rama and Hanuman in *The Ramayana*, as pictured on the walls of Descent of the Ganges in Mahablipuram, South India…

Position One: Stand with your feet flat on the ground with the head, neck, and trunk in a straight line; the feet should be as far apart as possible. Place the palms together in prayer position at the chest, and gently close the eyes. Stand silently, and engage in deep Ujjaya breathing.

Position Two: Raise the arms above the head, look up at the tips of your fingers, and hold. Breathe deeply in a deep, upward stretch.

Position Three: Bend back as far as possible, sliding the hands down the thighs.

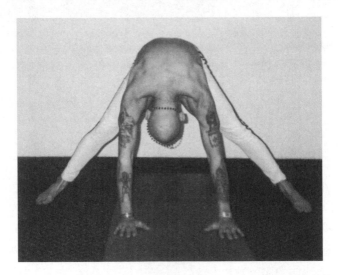

Position Four: Let the weight of gravity pull you forward, and slide your hands all the way down to your ankles.

Position Five: Pull back up, bringing the hands in prayer position, and slowly turn the right foot out, with the left foot still forward at ninety degrees. Now, bring your hands behind your back and bend back, bending your back knee, too.

Position Six: Bend forward at the hips, and bring the head to the right knee.

Position Seven: Reach over your head, and clap with your hands in prayer position. Bring your hands down into full warrior, with your right hand extended straight forward, and your back hand in the same plane of ecliptic. This is a forward lunge on your right knee.

Position Eight: Do a tai chi swoop through with your back hand, and bring your back foot forward, not taking it off the ground. Hands are straight out in front, and your consciousness is on your fingertips.

Position Nine: Allow the weight of your hands to pull you forward into a deep forward bend, with your hands and feet flat on the floor. Deep ujjaya breathing will pull the energy of the shakti deep inside the earth into your body. Reach down deep inside the earth with your fingers and your toes, and ground yourself. Draw in the power of the Divine Mother shakti, that fiery, volcanic energy, and pull it in through your hands and your feet. And now, draw that energy up through your body, touching your toes, knees, thighs, stomach, heart chakra, and throat chakra, and cupping your hands over your eyes…shoot your hands up over your head and back into Namaste, arms extended straight up over your head.

❈

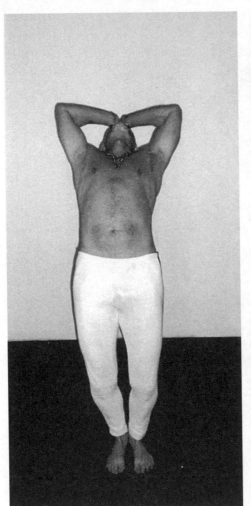 

Position Ten: Deep bend back with an inhalation, and now, bring the energy forward into Namaste at the heart chakra. Sit with this energy flow for a moment, and allow your new consciousness to emanate from your heart chakra.

❖

Daily Asana Regimen

Sarvangasana: Shoulder Stand

Lay flat on your back, with your hands at the sides, and raise up your legs to ninety degree position in alignment over your head, and now push on up to your shoulders with your hands, forming a tripod with your torso. You want your feet to be straight up, in a ninety degree angle with the floor. Keep adding time to this pose, until you can hold it for ten minutes.

Benefits: the benefits of the shoulder stand are incredible. It increases your circulation, and causes the blood to re-filter through the heart and inner organs by toning the thyroid. It helps to cure asthma, disorders of liver and intestines, hernia, diabetes, heart troubles, digestive problems, and will reduce abdominal fat. This is one of the most important yoga poses, and should be done daily. (Do not do this pose if you have a headache or fever. Breathing is short panting).

❖

Agnisara: Inner Fire

Stand with the feet apart. Keeping the spine straight, bend the knees slightly. Lean forward, placing your palms on your knees for balance. Exhale completely, and place the chin down on the hollow of the throat, holding your breath. Without inhaling, suck the abdominal muscles in and up, pulling in the naval to the spine. This creates a cavity inside the rib cage. Release, and then contract, the abdominal muscles five to ten times without inhaling…then, slowly inhale. Repeat this exercise two times.

Benefits: promotes health in all the internal organs, helps inner circulation in organs, stimulates digestion, and helps cure constipation and dyspepsia.

❈

Matsyasana: The Fish

Exhaling, lean back and set elbows on the floor for stability. Inhaling, arch the back, expand the chest, and place the crown of the head on the floor, arching upper back. Take hold of your big toes with index finger and thumbs, keeping the elbows on the floor. Breathing evenly, release tension in neck and shoulders. Now, release legs, and relax the body completely.

Benefits: provides a stretch to the cervical vertebrae. This exercise is a counter pose to Sarvangasana. It will eliminate the stiffness of the neck that might come from shoulder stand or head stands. The extended chest promotes good ventilation to the top of the lungs, increasing their capacity.

Ustrasana: The Camel Pose

Kneel, with the legs together. Exhaling, bend back from the waist, and place the palms on the soles of the feet. Hold for twenty seconds, breathing evenly.

Benefits: this pose brings flexibility of the spine, and good ventilation, increasing lung capacity.

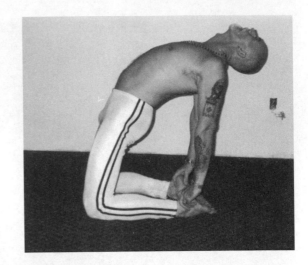

Natarajasana:
The King Dancer, Lord Shiva Pose

Exhaling, bend the left knee and grasp the instep of the foot with the left hand. Pull the foot as close to the buttocks as possible. Now, extend foot back into a full lunge. Finally, bring the foot forward into a uplifted Shiva Nataraja pose, with hands in opposing tira-pataka mudra. Gaze at a fixed point straight ahead, breathing evenly and hold for twenty seconds.

Benefits: this pose stretches the pelvic ligaments and develops poise balance and concentration.

Bhujapidasana: The Crow

Stand with the legs shoulder-width apart. Bend the knees, and place the palms on the floor, six inches apart. Spread the fingers for balance. Exhaling, lean forward, and place the upper thighs on the upper arms. Lift the feet from the floor, balancing the weight of the body on the hands. Point the toes, and draw them together until they touch. Breathe evenly, and hold for ten seconds. Lower the feet, and return to a standing pose.

Benefits: this pose strengthens your wrists and forearms, so that you can easily flow into the head stand. It also strengthens your abdominal and back muscles, and gives you better balance.

Simhasana: The Lion

Exhaling, open the mouth as wide as possible and thrust the tongue out and down trying to touch the chin. Gaze at a point between the eyebrows. Inhaling close the mouth and relax the face. Take one complete breath and repeat two more times.

Benefits: this pose makes the voice soft and melodious, releases headaches, takes away "lump in the throat," cures bad breath, and helps cure a sore throat.

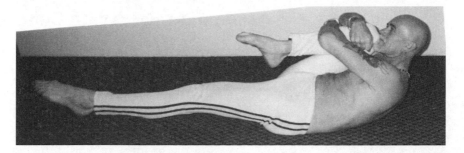

Aparnasana: Knee To Chest Pose

Lift your right foot six inches off the floor and bend at the knee into the chest, clasping with your hands. Lift your head up, and touch the nose to the knee as you also lift your left leg six inches off the floor. Toes are pointed downward. Hold this pose for twenty counts and with breath of fire. Then, alternate.

Benefits: this position opens the hip joints for detoxification. Also, it relieves flatulence and digestive problems, cures constipation, and increases endurance and stamina.

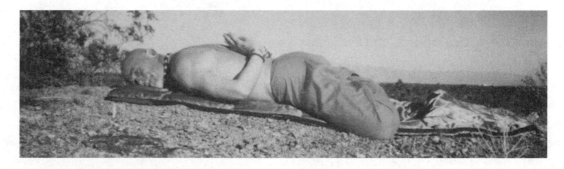

Lupta Padmasana: Hidden Lotus Pose

Sit in lotus position. Raise up on the knees, and bring the body forward, until the front of the legs, chest and chin are on the ground. Place hands behind the back in prayer position.

Benefits: this pose increases the flexibility of the hip joints.

Pranayama: Breath Control

Sitali, or the Cooling Breath: Fold the tongue lengthwise like a tube. Project the tip of the tongue outside of the mouth. Draw the air in through this tube with a hissing sound. Fill the lungs to capacity. Draw the tongue in, closing the mouth, and hold the air as long as possible. Exhale through the nose. Do three rounds.

Benefits: Sitali is a very easy way to cool the body. It helps remove heat, thirst, hunger and sleep.

Banarasana: Monkey Posture

Bend the left knee, with the foot flat on the floor. Make sure that the lower left leg remains perpendicular to the floor. Extend the right leg behind the body. Inhale, and raise the arms, bringing them high overhead in Namaste position. Look up at your hands as you move into a deeper lunge. Hold for ten counts, and then repeat on the opposite side.

Benefits: flexibility in the spine; stretches your pelvis; chest expands for deeper inhalation; strength. This is the pose Lord Hanuman practiced as he prayed to Rama before leaping to Sri Lanka in the Ramayana. The pose gave him the strength to do superhuman things!

Shirshasana: Headstand

Follow the instructions for the Crow position. Then, pull legs straight up into headstand. Spread the legs to form a "V," and rotate the ankles. Relax the feet. Breathe evenly, holding for thirty seconds. Bring the legs together.

Benefits: Considered the "King of Asanas" in Hatha Yoga; it is a panacea for all diseases. Increases the blood pressure and flow of blood to the brain. Brings exhilaration of spirit, and fills the body with energy. Increases memory and intelligence. Strengthens abdominal and lower back muscles.

Bathing and Purification

Bathing is very important to the yogi. Bathe as many times as you can a day. Bathing takes off bad vibes, and will clean your aura. When you bathe in the morning, say:

- Om Wak, and touch the water to your mouth
- Om Pran, and touch the water to your nose
- Om Shakshu, and touch the water to your eyes
- Om Strotam, and touch the water to your ears
- Om Shira, and touch the water to your head/mind
- Om Hridayam, and touch the water to your heart
- Om Shanti Shanti Shanti, and pour the water over your head with a water pot.

This is how you clean yourself for morning yoga, worship, and lighting incense at your home altar. GET CLEAN!

"You can't put the nectar in a dirty pot"

—Sri Anandamayi MA

Spiritual Clothes

Wear things that are satwic; wear things that flow. Wear clothes made of natural fibers, such as cotton, silk, and linen. When you wear light things, you will feel like you are covered by clouds. Wear a sari, and wear a khourta, and you will just love the way it feels. It is the perfect clothing for a spiritual life.

Be creative…let yourself go…be colorful…I think the reason why I love things from India is that almost everything is handmade. There is someone's energy in there, sewing all those tiny beads onto fabric, saying a mantra, and thinking of love. Now, that is something I can wear…LOVE.

Here is how to tie a sari:

Wrap the sari around your waist, and tie a knot at the end. Now, start pleating about every five inches, until you have made about ten pleats. Pull the remainder of fabric around your body, and over your shoulder. There are a lot of regional variations.

Here is how to tie a dhoti:

Tie the dhoti around your waist, in the center of the fabric. Make a knot. On the right side, make pleats, and fold them in the top over the knot. From the left side, pull the fabric between your legs, and fold it nicely, tucking it in the back like a diaper.

Also, everyone needs a chowdar. In India, both men and women wrap themselves at night with a wool shawl. Every yogi needs one.

photo by Saraswati

The ART of drinking CHAI

Yogis don't drink coffee. We drink chai. When you are in India…you will sip the nectar of the Gods even from the most grungy tea stall…fantastic chai! Chai is like a milk tea that is prepared with fantastic spices like cinnamon and cardamom. It has to be brewed with consciousness, love, and Bhava…otherwise, it's just tea, not chai. For you vegans out there (like me; I love you!), you can make it with soy milk, and it still tastes delicious. For you lazy folk out there who need your chai, but don't have the time to make it from scratch, there are a lot of brands now that are great and have a lot of love in them, like Oregon Chai.

Sharing Chai with spiritual friends (satsang!) is a must. Chai will inspire your thoughts and poetry. It will get you going on a cold morning. Drinking and preparing it is an artform. One cannot hang out in the Himalayas and be a yogi without CHAI!

Chai is India.

❖

Food For Thought...

Bengali Masar Dal

1 1/2 cups of red lentils
6 hot green chilies
1 teaspoon of tumeric
5 cups of water
1 teaspoon of salt
For flavoring the dal:
4 tablespoons of usli ghee
cup of minced onion
1 tablespoon of crushed ginger
1 cup of finely chopped tomatoes
For spice perfume dal
2 tablespoons of usli ghee
1 tablespoon of panch phoron mix
4 bay leaves
4 dry red chili pods
2 tablespoons of minced garlic

While the lentils are cooking, heat the Usli ghee in a large frying pan over medium heat, when it's hot add the onions and fry, stirring constantly. Add the ginger and tomatoes, and continue frying until cooked. Combine and cook lentils until done.

Swamiji's Daily Yoga Schedule

(For An Englightened Life…)

- Awaken at 5:00 a.m. for ritual bathing.
- Pranayama and chanting.
- Silent meditation.
- Yoga asanas.
- Breakfast…chai, fruit, oatmeal.
- Go to work.
- Lunch: salad, tofu, and miso; or dhal and chapatis.
- Rest quietly…or read a spiritual book.
- Back to work.
- Go home.
- Take your shoes off at the door (leave your worries outside!)
- Have some chai, and read something inspirational.
- Prepare dinner: salad, tofu, veggies, dhal and chapatis (food of the gods; it will keep you trim and in bliss!)
- Clean up.
- Evening meditation or bath, with beautiful music: devotional bhajans; classical; Indian, Western, or New Age.
- Resist one more day of turning on the television. Instead, opt to read Swami Sivananda's *Thought Power*.
- Write in your journal, play music, go to yoga class, dance, paint, or take a lovely evening walk with your kids and pets.
- Quietly light a candle in your room, and pray for peace.
- Blow out the candle, and slip into bed with your favorite stuffed Hanuman…and sleep and dream about MA!

❖

If you live this way, I guarantee BLISS! Each day will be like a beautiful pearl on an endless strand of priceless pearls. You will wake up every day, and say, "YES! Wow! One more day of a wonderful life! Thank you God, Thank you MA! Your life will be filled with Bhakti.

Everyone you meet will feel your Happiness.

You will not have wasted this human birth.

Happiness will follow you wherever you go.

My friends, what I am sharing with you comes from my Heart.

Ending Road Rage!

If you are spending every day in horrible road rage, running here and running there, and no one is moving fast enough for you, STOP! You are on a pathway that leads to destruction. The human body cannot handle those kinds of feelings on a constant, daily basis. We only have a few years here on Earth, so please sit down and breathe and take a personal reassessment of the situation. NOTHING and NO ONE and NO amount of money are worth hell on Earth!

I know you have to go to work. I know traffic is bad, but come on…you came from a beginningless beginning, and you are going to an endless end…why upset yourself so? You are an infinite being…how can there be any terror or fear when you are infinite!? You are consciousness, and you cannot kill consciousness. So slow down, settle down, and when you are in bad traffic and road rage, pick up your Japa Malas (yoga beads.)

Chant and Be Happy!

Here is a way out…a way to Bliss and Peace…take your beads, and take a breath of air…and relax.

Each bead is touched only with the thumb and third finger of the right hand. Your beads are God's name, so treat them with respect. Take your favorite name of God: RAM, Shiva, MA, Christ, Buddha, etc. Say, "OM RAM," Or "OM CHRIST," or "OM GOD"…each bead flows to the next bead. When you get to the bead with the tassel on it, that is the guru bead, that means to turn around and go back the other way! HA!

❖

This way, with each round of the beads, you will start to turn your life around, and with each round, I guarantee, you will feel better. You will feel bliss, and God's name will start to taste so sweet on your lips; the rage will fall away, and you will see that traffic really isn't that bad. And you will start to smile. You will think of me, and see that I am smiling back at you. Swami Ramananda is saying to you, "My friend, slow down; life really isn't that bad…and you have all of eternity to find your way…let go, and let God."

"OM NAMA SHIVAYA means not my will, Lord, but Thy will be done…"

—Sri Anandamayi MA

"The Journey of a thousand miles begins with one step."

—Lao Tzu

photo by Krishna Priya

Karma Yoga
The Yoga of Selfless Service to Humanity

"In this Kali Yuga, the greatest thing we can do with our lives is selfless service to humanity, or what I call Seva. Serve mankind with all the love in your heart, and work hard tirelessly for others, and your ego will rise no more. Put love into every step you take, and into every ounce of effort you make, and offer it all to Lord Shiva. Save nothing for yourself; give it all to God, and all of mankind, which is God. You will be blessed beyond measure; you will take Liberation."

—Babaji Maharaj of Gangotri

What is Karma Yoga? Karma Yoga is your spiritual work in this world. It can take many forms. It may be sweeping out an ashram kitchen. It may be clipping the lawn. It may be building a house. Karma Yoga is all those times you work with no thought of personal gain. You throw yourself into your work, chanting, "Sita Ram" all the way.

"Perhaps one of the greatest experiences of my life is working alongside Baba Hari Das, or Babaji, as we lovingly call him at Mt. Madonna. As you are working and building a house for someone, you can feel yourself receiving so much shakti. You have nails, boards, and hammers, and you start to work. Suddenly, you realize you are not even the one who is hammering. The silent sage smiles, and you can feel him working right through you. Eventually, there is a house, a home built of selfless service and love for one's community! If we all could just live this way! He shows us the way to give and give with no thought, except that of God. What a blessing it is, to perform seva around such a saint."

—Swami Ramananda

122

When I think of those beings who have given so much Karma Yoga, I think of Mahatma Ghandi; Dr. Martin Luther King, Jr.; Mother Teresa of Calcutta; The Mother of the Sri Aurobindo Ashram; the Reverend Cecil Williams of Glide Memorial Church in San Francisco; St. Francis of Assisi; and Jessica Simmons of Palm Springs, CA. I think of all the people who give and give, and who work so hard for others, in order to make this a better world. What lights! What shining examples of LOVE in this world!

Here is my exercise for you in Karma Yoga: try every single week to perform some selfless act for the benefit of humanity. It doesn't have to be grand. It can be as simple as cleaning out your closet and giving away clothes you don't wear to a worthwhile charity, or donating a few hours in a kitchen where homeless people are fed, or writing a check to go towards food for orphanages in India. Please don't miss the opportunity in life to do something nice for others. It will bless your life, and give you good KARMA.

> "You only really have what you give. If you can't give it, then you really don't
> have it. Those who give selflessly are the wealthiest persons on Earth."
>
> —Tat Wala Baba

Having a Sense of Humor is the Pathway to Finding Bliss!

No person I ever met had a better sense of humor than Sri Anandamayi MA. She could make us all laugh in an instant. She was always watching for that little slip to help us look at ourselves with humor. And when Mother laughed, it was infectious. You could not resist it, even if you could not understand what exactly She saw that was so funny. Mother would tickle your funny bone…and She would laugh until we had to fan Her and give Her water.

Now, there are laughing clubs all over the world. Even in India, large groups of people get together and laugh and laugh…it is a great yogic practice! Start your group today…or make everyone in your ashram get together for a laughing night. It may be the best thing you ever did for your life and your sadhana.

"We all need a sense of humor about ourselves; about this illusory world!"

—Sri Anandamayi MA

"I can't stop laughing at times. I just feel the joy trickling through my soul. How can you resist? Can't you see the tears in my eyes! Don't take this world or yourself so seriously…you are much sweeter when you laugh and don't get upset at life's ups and downs. Come, and laugh with me!"

—Swami Shankarananda Giri

"When you get so blue and life is beating you up, look at yourself in the mirror and honestly have a good chuckle. You will find a lot of strength in that laughter. See how beautiful your face looks when you are laughing. The world is full of miserable people, so please, don't be another one. Come and walk the mountain with me, and let's have a good laugh at life. I promise that you will feel better…and if you don't, I may just tickle you!"

—Swami Ramananda

I love being around my God brother, Bhagavan Das. We can't look at each other without laughing or crying or loving, because we are so much a reflection of one another. That joy of being with another spiritual being is just pure satsang. If he tells me about the ups and downs of his life, I just see him sitting in Tat Wala Baba's cave, where we both lived at times. The vibration of that cave was incredible. To share a cave with a God-being like Tat Wala Babaji! I always say, "Well, Baba, anything has to be better than that cave!" Then, we both smile and laugh, in order to put everything into perspective, and remember all of our good fortunes in life. Even the simplest form of living existence on this planet can be so beautiful. So, what is there to fear, when you know that you can even survive living in a cave? When I think about it, I feel an infinite gratitude for all I have in life; everything I have now is more comfortable than living in a cave! When one has this perspective, everything that comes your way in life is humorous and appreciable.

The more you soar in your meditations and practices, the higher you will become, and you will have easy access to the higher lokas, where you will find only BLISS. When you truly have the darshana of gods like Ganesha, Krishna, Shiva, Radha…you will find Them smiling and dancing. They will be so happy to see you as you come into Their holy presence. You will see Ganesha's humor. It is very important to cultivate this attitude toward life and to not take life too seriously. Then, you will be more God-like. I see people running about, beating themselves up with guilt and low self-esteem, and falling into all sorts of addictions. They live lives of misery and unhappiness. Some of the people I know are multimillionaires; they have so many homes, so many cars, and so many toys, and when I ask them if they are happy, they tell me emphatically, "NO!" I even had one very wealthy man in Palm Springs offer me all his wealth if I could give him happiness! This has to be cultivated; it can't be bought. A good sense of humor is the way. Try to see life like a child; Anandamayi MA was this way. She was so pure and innocent. She was happy, acting like a child when She would see you, and She would laugh at the slightest things. At life's seeming ups and downs, She would laugh. At life's temptations, She would laugh. At disappointments, She would laugh. There is only really GOD, and everything else in this illusory world is maya, so why get so down and disappointed? Kick up your heels, put on a costume, go say HI to strangers on the street, and smile at everyone! Then, the world will be a better place. Have fun with life!

Baba Hari Das wrote to me on his chalkboard: "We are lila sages playing in the forest. Come join us!"

"I attended a puja recently that Swami Ramananda gave in California. We all touched a fire, he put a red dot of kumkum on my forehead and I felt a very powerful shakti. I walked away from the puja, feeling powerful and alive, and deeply grateful to God. I was shopping at the market, and everyone was smiling at me. I thought to myself, 'Wow, I must have really received some powerful energy today!' I was swelling with pride. As I stood in line to purchase my groceries, everyone was looking into my eyes, and smiling and lifting their eyebrows. I really thought I was glowing or something. Then, on my way out of the market, I looked in a mirror, and realized that Swamiji had put a huge, bright red dot on

❈

125

my forehead! I laughed so hard all the way to the car! No wonder everyone was smiling at me! Every time my ego gets puffed up, Swamiji just makes me laugh at myself."

—Aditi Devi

Diet for a Spiritual Life

I always suggest that my students try to convert as much as possible to a vegetarian diet. First of all, as yogis, we take a vow in the Yamas and Niyamas of Ahimsa…which means to not kill any living creature. When we eat animals that have been brutally killed, we take on that vibration, and it becomes very hard to sleep at night. The violence you have eaten will play over and over in the food you have ingested.

I beg people to give vegetarianism a chance. Just try it for a month, see if you like it, and notice how you feel. Almost every vegetarian I know has the most gorgeous body, if they have also been practicing yoga. You, too, can look like a God or Goddess. The skin of vegetarians is so beautiful, and vegetarians look eternally young. They are at peace with the universe, harming no one and nothing to survive on this planet. This is the best way.

"The greatest singular thing that could bring change to this planet and great health to its people is a conversion to a vegetarian diet."

—Albert Einstein

Yogic Lifestyle

A yogi goes to bed early and rises early. I know this is a hard one for you night owls…but give it a chance, and see how you like it. It will become addicting. There is nothing like seeing the first rays of sun in the morning. The golden sun rises, and says, "Hello! Here I am again, and you have another wonderful day of life!" If you live your life in this spirit, you will always be happy. Bliss will shower upon you in infinite quantities.

❖

126

A yogi likes to go to sleep thinking gentle thoughts of peace. Read a great book on the pastimes of Lord Krishna…or poetry…listen to gentle, New Age music, or a light Sitar raga. Light candles in your room, and place jasmine flowers in a bowl next to the bed. Live your life with this kind of sensitivity and poetry…and you will turn into an angel of bliss.

There is so much unhappiness and turmoil in this world. Please don't be part of it. Here is an opportunity to live a lifestyle of peace and love.

"Live every day like it is a beautiful brush stroke on the canvas of life. Make every brush stroke on your canvas masterful and perfect. Live in that kind of

❖

127

peace and color. Put great stuff into your mind. Work only to help others, and hurt no one. Live a virtuous life, and sing God's praises all day long. At the end of your life, this canvas will be so masterful that you will be a LIGHT in a dark world. Become this, a master of the ART of LIVING."

—Dr. Hari Das Chaudhuri

Former President, California Institute
of Asian Study

The Yogic lifestyle is an important element in the steps leading to Bliss. First of all, make sure that your home has the right vibration. You should do arati with a brass plate full of flowers, incense, a camphor lamp, offerings of rice and sweets, and a holy picture of your Guru or favorite God. Take this plate, and offer it in a circular motion in every room of your house, and yes, even the closets and bathrooms. After consecrating your home, keep your house immaculate. This is very important for the bathrooms and kitchen. Make sure your clothes are hung properly, and give away any excess you have in order to keep the vibe pure and simple. Keep toilet seats down and closet doors closed at night for good Vastu Vidya. Keep your living space clean.

Then, start keeping yourself immaculate. Cleanliness is next to Godliness. Take lots of baths, as time permits. Always wear fresh, lightly flowing clothing. Use scented oils like sandalwood for aromatherapy. This is the beginning of your experience of heaven on Earth…treat yourself to beautiful baths and nice, flowing clothes. Give all the black gothic stuff away; that belongs to another time period, and you don't need any negativity in your life.

Next, start regulating the music in your life. Live with beautiful sitar music, or New Age music. Listen to bhajans, or devotional music, all day long. You will start living in a wonderful space, and the atmosphere will take you right into peace. If you are watching awful violent television shows all day long, or talk shows on which everyone is fighting and screaming, that is the vibration you are bringing into your home.

Your home is a temple. Would you scream and shout and act violently in a temple? Of course not. Don't allow it in your home. Instead, listen to beautiful music, do flower arrangements, read poetry, and read books that inspire you spiritually. One of my yoga students only reads wonderful children's books, and she says that they keep her happy. That is certainly okay for a devotee of Anandamayi MA, who called Herself "only a child" all the way through life. Mother felt if we always stayed in a close relationship with our inner child, we could remain pure and innocent throughout life.

Once you have created this holy atmosphere, start watching your thoughts. Now is the real sadhana, or spiritual practice. Make your thoughts focused, peaceful, loving and pure. Don't let anyone or anything pull you out of your purity. If you only think beautiful thoughts, the whole atmosphere of your home will shine, like a beautiful ashram.

Use discrimination now about who and what you bring into your space. In Vedanata, we call this "iti iti and neti neti," or this and not that! As a Swami, I recommend that you do not allow the following things into your home:

+ shoes (they spread a lot of disease and bacteria; if you are doing a yoga practice on the floor, you should especially not allow shoes to be worn in your home.)
+ smoking (causes cancer and a low unspiritual vibration, because it harms yourself and others.)
+ meat (the vibration of the violence of how the animal is killed is contained in the meat, and it is a low vibration.)
+ drugs (drugs are tamasic, or low energy. A yogi is in natural bliss, and needs no crutches or artificial highs.)
+ alcohol (tamasic, low energy and harms the liver.)
+ loud, violent cursing or swearing; foul language; or foul thoughts (they lower the vibration, and chase away the peace.)
+ guns or weapons (they invite disaster; read Alan Hunter's *Courage in Both Hands*, and live without fear.)
+ violent or upsetting books or movies (just their presence on the shelf can cause a bad vibration.)

Use your gut instinct, and toss anything that doesn't ring pure and with your heart of truth out of your environment.

❈

129

Now, your house is clean and wonderful, like a temple or an ashram. Go to your altar, light some candles, light some incense…sit in that wonderful spiritual presence you have created and feel the peace…AHHHHHHHHHHH! Okay, now it's time to do an inner housecleaning.

Open a window in your heart chakra, and let go of anything you are holding inside that is upsetting you…grudges, hurt, envy, jealousy, sadness, etc. Let it all go out that window. Every time you let go of something, just release some more and release some more. This way, you will start to feel so light, and you will start to smile again. You will feel so happy that nothing and no one will be able to bring you down. Even go back to your childhood, and start forgiving everyone who has ever hurt you.

> "Forgiveness is the greatest housecleaner in the world. Would you like for your house to be clean and light? Then FORGIVE everyone…"

—Swami Shankarananda Giri

> "The more I forgive, the more I find myself in the waterfall of unconditional love. From this posture of pure love, with no expectations of other human beings, you are free from hurt, fear, and jealousy. You just live in love and bliss. The ticket to bliss is forgiveness."

—Swami Ramananda

And now, in your inner housecleaning, open a window in your Mind. Start releasing those thoughts that are judgemental. Release those thoughts that want to get you ahead in life at the expense of others (get rid of these immediately; they invite really bad karma). Release thoughts of manipulating others for your own personal gain. Let go of those thoughts that try to control others. Throw all those thoughts of low self-esteem and self-destruction out the window. Now, just open the window really wide, and let everything go out…do a full housecleaning up there in the mind. I guarantee that you will feel so much better; you will feel so much happier and lighter.

Now, let the pure Light radiate in your mind. Just stay empty beyond thoughts, beyond knowledge, and beyond your ego. Suddenly, the bliss will start to pour into your mind, like the

❖

first rays of a morning sunrise. Let Truth and purity stream into your mind. Just stay there, empty, and open, and surrendered. Now pray this prayer:

"Oh my dear God, All that I am, and all that I have, are yours. Make me an instrument of Thy Peace, Love, and Happiness in this world."

I promise you, your life will change. After this exercise, you will never be the same. A consciousness will flow into you. People will recognize it, and everyone on the street will be smiling at you. Strangers will come up and greet you, and they will tell you they feel your wonderful energy. You will start to just live in the Now, and you will be free. Friends will flock to your doorstep just to feel a little bit of your peace.

You will be a light in the world. Everything you do or say will be blessed. You will become a master of the art of living. I am speaking from experience: this is the world I live in every moment of every day, my friends, and it is wonderful!

"BE HERE NOW. Okay, we're here now. Now, we want BLISS. Let's find some Happiness in this world. Bhakti is the way…BLISS NOW!"

—Swami Ramananda

"Yogic lifestyle is utterly important. If you are going to talk the talk, you had better walk the walk, and that means living it twenty-four hours a day, seven days a week. A yogi is there in the moment, walking around high on life, dynamic, in the now, awake, and living life in higher consciousness. You can't fake it. It's gotta be real."

—Mike Santeros, Yoga Teacher, Los Angeles

"So what are you going to do? All your friends are heading to the donut shop, and you are a yogi! I listen to my body, and my body says, 'No, I don't want that junk in me, I just got clean!' 'Great,' I say, as I pull out my spring water and hang with the gang without judgement. I only feel happy that I am receiving such inner guidance."

—Michelle Cohen, Yoga Student, NYC

"I brought Swami Ramananda to my house in Palm Springs. He walked into one room, and said, 'What do you do in this room?' I was very embarrassed to tell him that it used to be my playroom in my sexual heyday. He said, 'Meditate and pray here, and make it your temple.' I draped the walls with beautiful tapestries. I moved in a Chinese table I found, and placed an incredible Buddha from Thailand there. Swamiji came and blessed the room, and showed me how to consecrate the room to Lord Buddha. Since we changed that one room, the vibration in my whole house has changed. Now, everyone wants to sit in that room and feel the peace."

—Michael David, Yoga Student, Palm Springs

photos by *Sudama*

"In times of disaster and challenge like 9/11…I say to never take your eyes off the LIGHT. Pray, pray, and more give more prayer. Pray for peace and enlightenment for this planet. Pray that we can build a world where our children will be happy, safe, and free. Pray for your enemies, that they can find love, and that their hearts will drain of hate and envy. Pray that every misguided, violent killer on this planet can find the Light and Transform. Pray that all of us can reach out to one another and hug one another without fear, and with the knowledge that we all are Divine Beings, sharing a beautiful planet in Space. Oh, my friends, never stop praying…those prayers are affirmations, and they come true."

—Swami Ramananda

SATSANG: Creating a Spiritual Community

In the Bhagavad Puranas, God tells us the way He best loves to be worshiped. Number one is Music and Singing, Number two is Dancing, and Number three is ART! There is nothing like gathering with friends and getting a guitar, or harmonium and tablas, and letting those bhajans rip! One day recently, I sang bhajans all day long with Jai Uttal, and by the end of the day, we were all so high we could barely walk. We were laughing and crying, all at the same time. You see, the songs just open your heart, and when you sing to God…She just pulls you up to Her bosom, loves you, and caresses your soul.

When you sing with Bhagavan Das, you just want to soar and dance and cry out to Krishna, "Thank you God for giving me this life!" When you hear Krishna Das sing with that deep steady voice of his, you feel like you are flowing within the Ganges itself, and that your heart and soul are just washed clean with God's holy name.

This is the power of kirtan. This is the power of singing God's name. It doesn't matter if you are in a black Baptist Church and singing out to Jesus; or if you are a sufi, swirling and crying, "Allah Akbar;" or if you are in a Krishna Temple dancing to "Hare Krishna, Hare Rama"…it's all the same, and God is listening. You are loving Him and worshipping Him with your songs, much like the birds on the mountain do every day.

❈

photo by Radha

My Guru, Anandamayi MA, loved singing, and She sang beautifully! Oh, how I loved to hear Mother sing with so much JOY! She was showing us the way…the path of Bhakti, how to let our hearts go in Song and just give every drop of Love to God.

How to Sing a Bhajan

Pick something simple like "Jai Ram, Sri Ram"…sing it over and over, and make up a nice tune…call and response…slip into the Bhava…"Govinda jaya jaya, Gopala jaya jaya, Radha Ramanahari Govinda Jaya Jaya." First you sing, and then the bhaktas sing…back and forth. Don't read the words; feel them in your heart. Let them sing out of your heart, and they will purify your mind. OM Namah Shivaya…"Thy will be Done"…SING WITH ALL YOUR HEART…you will find bliss.

❖

happy people don't fight!

ENLIGHTENMENT

Lord Ramachandra and Sita Devi

❉

My Invitation...

This can be a wonderful life, but you have to make the choice to live it that way. YOGA is the way. It will save your life, and keep you young and healthy. My friends, life is so short. Please don't waste this life. A human birth is so precious, and so difficult to attain. Even the gods line up in heaven to take a human birth on Earth, because it is the way to achieve Samadhi, Enlightenment. If you feel lost, please find me. Come and walk the Sun-lit path with me, and let us laugh, love, and have Satsang together! Believe me, it is the greatest thing you can do with your life. If you need a Guru, a great and wonderful guide, may I suggest Sri Anandamayi MA? She is for everyone, and She loves you ALL! There is HOPE! Find ME...I love you! JAI MA!

—Swami Ramananda

"Yogis are different people. A yogi wants liberation."
— Sharon Gannon, Jivanmukti Yoga, NYC

You can see a yogi on the street. He walks softly. Each foot step is a prayer of thanks to the Divine Mother. He doesn't stomp around like a herd of buffalo. He walks gently, as if on a cloud, because he experiences yoga with the earth, and the earth is a goddess. A yogi talks differently, because he doesn't want to throw negative energy out into the universe…he doesn't want to do anything that would hurt his sadhana.

A yogi holds himself upright at all times, because he wants to feel the kundalini shakti. He is experiencing yoga with his body, and the more the body gets pure and becomes a temple…the more it guides you into what it truly needs.

One of my students was reading books about the scandals of saints and the shortcomings of gurus. He came to me, all filled with negativity, and was going to leave his path, because no one was perfect. I said, "You know, they are all in a human body; did you really expect even a saint to be perfect? It's not going to happen in the Kali Yuga. Why are you wasting your time with such negative gossip? Instead, you need bhakti, devotion, and inspiration. If you dig deeply enough into anyone's past, you will find dirt. Why not look at a teacher and take what they really stand for; take the greatest things they have ever said and done, and hold that close to your heart?"

I was intimately close to Anandamayi Ma, and to all of the gurus of India, and I never saw Her in one scandal or shortcoming. She was as pure as they come. A reporter came from New Delhi, and he was trying to trap Ma with questions of Her past. He said She was illiterate, and claimed that she only like Bhamans. Ma sat, looking at him with total love. She loved everyone, and She didn't care if you were Muslim, Jew, Christian, Hindu…that you loved God was all She really cared about. She blessed him, and turned to all of us, and said, so eloquently and so sweetly:

"Unvarying tranquility will always triumph over sarcasm."

The Divine Mother is just love, and emptiness…a perfect mirror of the best part of ourselves. Mother looked at me, and saw God. Because She saw the divine part of me, She called that forth. As a result, I saw my own divinity, and I merged with truth.

"Bhava will lead you to mahabhava, and mahabhava will lead you to prem (pure love.)"

— Sri Anandamayi Ma

When you get discouraged,
and you are ready to quit
your yoga practice,
you look up,
and there is Ma,
loving you so patiently
and so completely…

Put your heart and soul into your yoga practice…yoga should take us into consciousness. Perform each asana with bhakti, smiling, and at the end of each asana, say "swaha!"

"Proportionate to your quest for God, your evolution, is God's grace. So as you reach up and evolve and transform, God is reaching down and giving you His grace, or involution."
Evolution = Involution, so never give up hope!
—Sri Aurobindo

Once, in Deradune, MA asked me to sing a bhajan. We were sitting serenely on the grass in front of the house. I looked up at the beautiful Himalayan sky, and launched into singing "OM Nama Shivaya!" We sang our hearts out, and it was so beautiful.

At the end of the song, MA turned sweetly to me and said, "That was beautiful Ramananda, and now, can you tell me what "Om Nama Shivaya" means?"

"Thank you, Mother. I believe it means that God's name is Shiva."

"That is right, but even more so, we sing this song with total surrender. Its true implication is, 'THY WILL BE DONE'".

After Mother's explanation of Om Nama Shivaya, I will always sing that powerful mantra with a new understanding.

photo by Sudama

❖

"How much more time will you spend at a wayside inn? Don't you want to go home? How exquisite it all is…One is, in his own Self, the wanderer, the exile, the home coming and the home…oneself is all that there is…"

—Sri Anandamayi Ma

"If life beats you up, and everywhere you turn is just another block…and you start to despair and really think of just ending it all…please think of me. I am here for you, and I am filled with love for you. I am holding onto your hand in the quicksand, and I am not going to let you sink. Take a deep breath, and realize that, no matter how bad it gets, you are going to make it. Love conquers All. My love for you is Infinite."

—Swami Ramananda

"MA told us about the Kali Yuga and how difficult and challenging the times ahead would be. She said that the greatest way to survive and stay on the path is through satsang. Satsang is the association of enlightened spiritual friends, so watch who you hang out with, and try to hang out with the saints. When I am with my buddies like Bhagavan Das and Jai Uttal, for example, we just look into each other's eyes and fall into bliss, and we realize that it's really Neem Karoli Baba and Anandamayi Ma looking at one another… that is pure satsang!"

—Swami Ramananda

"We may not be enlightened, but we can talk about it! This is satsang; we're having satsang!"
—Sharon Gannon, Jivanmukti Yoga, NYC

"When I get to hang out with Swami Ramanada, we walk on the mountain together and laugh. There are usually maybe just five of us, but I really just feel so good to be near him and hear his laughter. Sometimes, we talk about spiritual things, like the difficulties we are having, but most of the time, we just hang together, and we just sit on the top of the mountain and breathe. We look out at the beautiful desert below, and I feel so good that I could fly! I just want to be near him, and near others who so deeply love God. I think it's the most important thing in life. I know this is satsang, and it really helps me stay with my sadhana, and I feel like now I know bliss…"
—Saraswati, Yoga Student

"Swami Ramananda is the happiest man I have ever met. His joy is infectious and addicting, and it is a wonderful addiction."
—Allen Ginsberg

"Swamiji is one of the closest friends I have ever had to being a brother. I feel happy just to be near him…"
—Tony Curtis

"Satsang is hanging out with the enlightened ones. My whole journey in India was satsang."

—Baba Bhagavan Das

SHUKRJA!

A special thanks to my dear devotees and friends who have given me so much support in this project. Thank you and God bless you: Swami Swarupananda, Aleta, Bill & Cheryl Gladstone, Kenzi, Shraddha Ma, Dianne Lynn, Nate Sudama, Bhakti Rasa, Audrey Peacock, Amita, Sita, Janaki Devi and Ganga Ram Deva, Nancy and Karolyn and Aunt Marge, Mandakani, Saraswati, Saras and Rasa, Kelly Breaux, Bharti Ma, the Pathak family, Prem Das and Tara Devi, and all of my darling children at the Jai Ma Ashram in Rancho Mirage and the Palm Desert Yoga Center. I love all of you! Jai Sita Ram!

I also would like to extend a very special thanks to Baba Ram Dass for the gift of light he is to the entire American spiritual community. He opened the door to the West in so many ways with his book, *Be Here Now*; gave so many years of tireless seva; and loved my Guru, Sri Anandamayi MA. Thank you, my dear friend.

You've Got to Have Friends...

To my dear friends who are such rays of light to me: Bhagavan Das, Jai Uttal, Geoffrey, Sharon Gannon and David Life, Amita MA, Tony Curtis and Jill Melody Thomas, Cynthia Sykes, Goldie Hawn, and the whole gang at Yoga House Hollywood, to Daya Mata, Amachi MA, Guru Mai, Baba Hari Das, Alice Coltrane Swamini: you all have my greatest respect and love forever...

AND

There would not be *Bliss NOW* without the Lotus Feet of Sri Sri Anandamayi MA, or Sri Swami Shankarananda Giri...the loves of my life.

❖

Time Alone...
The Journey Inward, The Final Journey

"Oftentimes, I will drive Highway One in California, up the dramatic and infinitely beautiful coastline to Big Sur. Here, you will find abandoned beaches on which you can walk for miles and never see another soul. Here, the mountains and redwood forests meet the churning sea. Here, cascading waterfalls drop some four hundred feet, from redwood forests into the crashing sea. Huge monolithic rocks stand like timeless Shiva lingams and withstand the assault of each drenching wave. I go to these places of solitude, and walk the beach alone, for many miles. Sometimes, I build a fire, and sit alone, pondering the myriad heavenly stars, while the waves crash against the rocks on the shoreline. What a celebration it is, to be with my Self. What a tremendously golden experience it is to just share such a bright moment of being alone with God. I savor the quiet, the peace, the meditation…with no fear, just happiness, and an undeniable, golden Presence.

Some people say it is a curse to be so seemingly alone in such an austere place. I say, my friends, it is the Way. This is the truth I found in India, alone in a cave in the Himalayas. Once you find that space of peace, of trust, of faith…your heart and mind will flood with Light. Once you are truly quiet, your mind is silent. Ahhhh, there it is: GOD IS HERE…and that light will shine on your inner treasure, on the presence of God within your own soul.

❀

The journey inward is the only journey worth traveling in this world, but it takes a long time to see that. I think that you must travel the world and really live a lot in the outer world to get to that place. And finally, there is peace, and it really is okay just to be alone with your Self. It's really okay to love your Self. And when you find it, and you start to see that golden inner glow, your life turns into a supernova. All the bright moments of your life start to pass in dancing bubbles of happy memories. All the love and compassion you have given falls back on you like a divine boomerang, and your heart just sails into BLISS. You see and start to live in the Divine part of your being, and everything else in life appears mundane.

This book only has one purpose. My wish for you is a life of peace and happiness. To spread this joy is the only purpose of my life. Now that I have found it, and live in this eternal bliss, I want you to experience it too.

Oh, won't you walk this silvery path with me? Don't waste this beautiful, earthly life on unhappy dramas and unholy trivialities. Come and share the poetry of Being. Let your heart soar like the seagull. Sing your prayers of peace and love. Be a bright beacon of Truth and Joy. Thank you for giving me the time to speak to your heart…and know that as you walk this journey, you are never alone. I am right here, walking alongside you. We are eternal beings, and I will hold your hand in Spirit forever."

Jai Ma,
Swami Ramananda
om shanti, shanti, shanti, om

BLISS NOW!

BLISS NOW!

BLISS NOW!

BLISS NOW!

BLISS NOW!

BLISS NOW!

❖

books and internet sites
to nourish the soul

Goddess Saraswati

❖

books that nourish the soul

Anandamayi Ma the Mother Bliss-Incarnate, by Anil Ganguli Sri Anandamayi Charitable Society

A Classical Dictionary of Hindu Mythology and Religion, by John Dowson Rupa & Co., New Delhi

Ashtanga Yoga Primer, by Baba Hari Das Sri Rama Publishing, Santa Cruz

Autobiography of a Yogi, by Paramhansa Yogananda, Self-Realization Fellowship Press

Benares City of Light, by Diana L. Eck, Princeton University Press

Be Here Now, by Baba Ram Dass, Hanuman Foundation

Bhagavad Gita, by Swami Sivananda, Divine Life Society Press

Bliss Divine, by Swami Sivananda, Divine Life Society Press

Dancing with Shiva, by Subramuniyaswami, Himalayan Accademy Books

Devotional Passages from the Hindu Bible, by Dhan Gopal Mukerji, Rupa & Co. Publishing, New Delhi

Endless Wisdom, by Swami Turiyasangitananda, The Vedantic Press

Flowers and Their Essences, by the Mother, Sri Aurobindo Society Press

From Here to Nirvana, by Anne Cushman and Jerry Jones Riverhead Books

From Sweeper to Saint, by Baba Hari Das, Sri Ram Books, Mt. Madonna

From the Life of Sri Anandamayi Ma, by Bithika Mukerji, Sri Anandamayi Charitable Society Book Trust

Gods and Goddesses of India, by B. K. Chaturvedi

❖

Hindu India, by Henri Steirlin Taschen

Illuminations from the Bhagavad Gita, by Chris Murray and Kim Murray, Mandala Books

India, by Martin Hurlimann, Viking Press

In Her Perfect Love, by Shraddha Davenport Patel, Shadakar Inddobhai Ipcowala Charitable Book Trust

Integral Yoga, by Dr. Haridas Chaudhuri, California Institute of Asian Study

Integral Yoga, by Swami Satchidananda Holt, Rinehart and Winston

It's Here Now, Are You?, by Bhagavan Das, Broadway Books, NY

Japa Yoga, by Swami Sivananda, Divine Life Society Book Trust, Rishikesh, India

Kena Upanishad, by Sri Aurobindo, Sri Aurobindo Society Book Trust

Khumba Mela by Jack Hebner and David Osborn, Entourage Publishing, Ganesh Editions

Lord Shiva and His Worship, by Swami Sivananda, Divine Life Society Book Trust

Loving Ganesha, by Subramuniyaswami, Himalayan Accademy

Matri Darshan, by Mangalam Verlag, Germany

Matri Vani, by Sri Anandamayi MA, Sri Anandamayi Charitable Society

Meeting God, by Stephen Huyler, Yale Univ.Press

The Mind of the Cells, by the Mother, Institut de Recherches Evolutives, Paris

Miracles of Love, by Baba Ram Dass, Hanuman Foundation

Monumental Eternal, by Swami Turiyasangitananda, The Vedantic Press

Mother as Revealed to Me, by Bhaiji Sri Anandamayi Charitable Society, Kankal

The Mother, by Sri Aurobindo, Sri Aurobindo Society Book Trust

Myths of Indian Art and Civilization, by Heinrich Zimmer, Bollingen Series, Princeton University

Mystic Monkey, by Baba Hari Dass, Sri Rama Publishing

Sadhus, by Dolf Hartsuiker, Inner Traditions

Savitri, by Sri Aurobindo, Sri Aurobindo Society Book Trust

Sad Vani, by Sri Anandamayi MA, Sri Anandamayi Charitable Society

Speaking of Siva, by A. K. Ramanujan, Penguin Books

Svakriya Svarasamrita, by Brahmcharini Kumari Chandan Puranacharya, Eastern Publishers, New Delhi

The Adventure of Consciousness, by Satprem, Sri Aurobindo Book Trust Pondicherry 2, India

❖

The Heart of Yoga, by T.K.V. Desikarchar, Inner Traditions
The Heart's Secret Door, by Swami Ramananda, Swami Ramananda Book Trust, Rishikesh, India
The Life Divine, by Sri Aurobindo, Sri Aurobindo Ashram
The Only Dance There Is, by Baba Ram Dass, Anchor Books
The Presence of Shiva, by Stella Kramrisch, Princeton University Press
The Upanishads, by Sri Aurobindo, Sri Aurobindo Book Trust, Pondicherry, India
The Vastu Vidya Handbook, by Juliet Pegrum, Three Rivers Press, NY
The Yoga Tradition, by Georg Feurerstein, Hohm Press
Vastu Living, Creating a Home For the Soul, by Kathleen Cox, Marlowe and Co. NY
Yoga Asanas, by Swami Sivananda, The Divine Life Society
Yoga Basics, by Yoga Journal, Henry Holt and Co. NY
Yogic Cures for Common Diseases, by Dr, Phulgenda, Sinha Orient Paperbacks, Hydrabad, India

great internet sites to visit

http://www.anandamayi.org
Anandamayi Ma Biography & links

http://www.bluedove.com/anandamayi.html
Blue Dove Press; books about Anandamayi Ma

http://www.miraura.org/
The Integral Yoga of Sri Aurobindo and the Mother, with links to the Ashram and Auroville

http://www.SivanandaDlshq.org
The Divine Life Society/Sivananda Ashram home page

http://www.himalayanacademy.com/
Hinduism Online

http://www.heartspace.org/
Excellent pictures and ideas for visits to India

http://www.hindunet.org
the Hindu Resource Center

http://www.pondy-central.com
Pondicherry Central

http://instantkarmastore.com/newsletter/features/ramananda1.html
Instant Karma Newsletter

http://www.alkhemy.com/sanskrit/dict/
Online Sanskrit Dictionary

http://www.hindu.org
Hindu Web Site

http://www.ILoveYoga.net
Swami Ramananda's New Life Yoga International Site

Glossary of Sanskrit Words

Goddess Maheshasurmardni

❖

A

AHIMSA—a vow of non-violence taken in Raja yoga, the path of Mahatama Ghandi; is a reason for vegetarianism.

ANANDAMAYI MA—the greatest female saint of India. She is considered by her devotees to be Avatara of Narayana. The guru of Swami Ramananda.

AMMACHI MA—a mother saint from Kerala who travels the world, giving Her shakti through hugs.

ARATI—the waving of a lighted flame before a deity in the Hindu puja. Flame symbolizes sense, elements, planets; one touches the flame for a blessing.

ASANA—seat; a yoga posture in the Hatha tradition.

ASHIRBAD—blessing from a guru; grace.

ASHRAMA—a spiritual hermitage; a monastic retreat.

ASHTANGA YOGA—eight-limbed path of discipline and restraint taught by Patanjali. Power Yoga.

ASHUTOSH—one of the names of Lord Shiva in His most gracious giving aspect; kindness.

ATMAN—God within; the divinity of the Individual Soul.

ATMANANDA—a female companion of Anandamayi MA.

AVATAR—a living incarnation of God in human form.

AVIDYA—ignorance.

B

BABA—Brother; usually refers to a holy man, saint, or sadhu; a respective title.

BABAJI—the "ji" is a respective title, like Sir. Many saints have this name, including the famous Babaji of the Himalayas, who has appeared for thousands of years.

BAKSHISH—gift. Children and beggars call this out in India wanting spare change, alms, or candy.

BHAKTI YOGA—the yoga of devotion.

BHAJAN—devotional music; singing of holy songs.

BHAVA—overflowing spiritual emotion or love.

BHUJANASANA—the cobra position.

❈

BLAVATSKY, MADAME—the founder of the Theosophical Society; a great occult mystic of the 20th century.

BRAHMACHARYA—student on the path; a celibate.

BRAHMA—creator of this physical world.

BRAHMAN—the ultimate reality, or Supreme Soul.

C

CHAKRAS—wheels of energy; seven vortices in the body.

CHAPPALS—Indian sandals, usually having a wooden sole and a strap holding the foot or any sandal.

CHAI—a milk tea made with many spices. Chai is the main drink of India for breakfast, and throughout the day.

CHELA—student disciple.

CHILLUM—an earthen pipe for smoking Ganga.

CHOWDAR—a long shawl worn by both men and women, sometimes cashmere, which is covered with gods or Sanskrit phrases.

D

DAL—lentils with many spices, eaten as the staple in India with chapatis. Perfect food.

DARSHAN—the viewing of a guru or holy person; sitting in their presence and energy.

DHARMA—your duty in life.

DHARMASALA—a Buddhist monastery.

DHOTI—a long cloth, about fifty inches long, wrapped like a diaper and worn by men traditionally in India, about fifty inches long.

DHUNDA—the stick of a holy man; a long stick covered with saffron cloth signifying a sanyasa.

DHYANA—yoga of mental constructions; meditation.

DIDI MA—Anandamayi MA's mother.

DRAVIDIAN—the ancient Tamil culture of South India; probably the oldest culture of India.

DREADLOCKS—or jatas; long locks of matted hair worn by a sadhu, symbolizing the overcoming of vanity, and wound on top of the head in the style of Lord Shiva.

❈

G

GANESHA—the elephant-headed god; remover of obstacles and the son of Lord Shiva. He is prayed to first before all other gods.

GANGA—the river Ganges; a goddess.

GHATS—stairways running down an embankment to a river, usually the Ganges, for the purpose of bathing.

GHOPURAM—the entryway towers of a South Indian temple, many stories high, and carved with deities.

GOPI—a milkmaid devoted to Lord Krishna.

GURU—teacher; spiritual guide.

GURU MAI—the leader of Siddha yoga, and Muktananda's successor; a great, living MA.

GURU PRIYA DEVI—Anandamayi MA's longtime caretaker and companion.

H

HARI—a name for the God Vishnu.

HATHA YOGA—physical postures for enlightenment.

HRIDAYAM—the heart chakra; your soul heart.

HANUMAN—The Hindu god of Strength and devotion; he is half-man and half-monkey; he is also the hero of *The Ramayana*.

I

ISHATA—the primary god you worship.

ISHWARAPRANIDAM—using your life force in the search for God. The yoga of finding your higher power; one of the three aspects of the Yoga Sutra.

J

JAI MA—victory to the Mother; a greeting used by all devotees of MA to anyone they meet.

JAPA YOGA—the yoga of repetition of God's name using your malas.

❈

JATAS—dreadlocks; symbol of a sadhu.

JIVANMUKTI—a liberated Soul; the mother ship of all yoga centers in New York City.

JNANA YOGA—the yoga of philosophy and knowledge.

K

KALI—a ferocious goddess form of Shiva. She eats the cesspool of our minds.

KALI YUGA—the current time period. A yuga cycle is 250,000 years. During this cycle, Kali is calling forth all of the vice and corruption of our minds.

KARMA—the law of cause and effect resulting from your actions: as you sow, so shall you reap.

KARMA YOGA—the yoga of selfless service.

KHEYALA—Anandamayi Ma's shakti and energy force.

KHOURTA—a tunic shirt worn by men over pajama style pants.

KHUMBA MELA—an astronomical festival occurring every twelve years when the planets all align, and millions bathe in the Ganges in Haridwar, Allahabad, or Nasik. Bathing on that day purifies all sins of all previous incarnations.

KIRTAN—repetition in song of God's name and holy phrases, sung with call and response.

KRISHNA—an incarnation of the god Vishnu; highly loved personality of God.

KUNDALINI—energy at the base of your spine, symbolized as a serpent, which brings shakti.

L

LIKHIT JAPA—the writing of God's names over and over.

LILA—play; often the playtime of Lord Krishna and his friends like hide and seek; a guru playing with you.

LINGAM—a phallic symbol of Lord Shiva, oftentimes a stone which is worshiped as the creative energy of Shiva. The principal phallic of a Shiva Temple.

LAKSHMI—goddess of wealth, and also regarded as money.

LOKA—a spiritual, heavenly world.

M

MA—Mother.

MAHABHAVA—a great outpouring feeling of emotion and love for God, or your Guru.

MAHABALIPURAM—a seaside city in Tamil Nadu, where 4,000 year old temples line the beaches.

MAHARAJI—great king; a respective title given to gurus; devotees' name for Neem Karoli Baba.

MAHASAMADHI—great sleep; when a guru passes into a higher state of nirvana, leaving the body, yet still remaining a presence within the body, even after death.

MALA—beads used for chanting and japa. Usually made of sandalwood, neem, tulsi or rudraksha beads.

MANASIKA—offering worship of a God on a mental level by visualising your offering with your mind.

MANGALARATI—morning puja, which starts at 4:00 a.m. with arati meditation, yoga, and bhajans.

MANTRA—Sanskrit words of powers, phrases which bring powers, enlightenment, protection, etc.

MAYA—illusion; this physical world.

MAUNA—a silent sage.

MOKSHA—liberation from the wheel of existence.

MUDRA—a symbolic hand gesture of finger expression to activate prana, or to communicate bhava.

MURTI—likeness of a god or a guru; could be a statue, or a large photo, or any likeness used in worship.

MUHLBANDHA—the closing of the anal sphincter.

N

NAGAS—snake deities, which are half-snake, half-human.

NAMASTE—the translation of hello in India. "I salute the light in you."

NADA YOGA—the yoga of inner sounds.

NADI—nerve channels.

NEEM KAROLI BABA—a great guru with many siddhis. The guru of Ram Dass, featured in *Be Here Now*.

NIRVAKALPA SAMADHI—a high super-conscious state invoked through meditation, in which one merges in Brahman.

NIRVANA—the state of being one with all that exists.

O

OM—the primal sound behind all of creation, GOD.

P

PADMASANA—sitting posture where the feet are crossed at the ankles and above the thighs.

PANDIT, PUNDIT—a greatly-taught person.

PARAMHANSA YOGANANDA—author of *Autobiography of a Yogi,* in which he wrote about MA. He was also Founder of Self-Realization Fellowship, the devotees of whom we consider our "spiritual cousins."

PITAJI—Anandamayi Ma's husband. She was married at the age of thirteen and he became her greatest devotee.

PRANA—life force in the air we breathe.

PRANAM—bowing with hands in Namaste; giving respect or obeisance to a teacher, or to anyone.

PRANAYAM—breathing techniques controlling prana.

PRASHADUM—food offered to God first, consecrated, and then shared afterwards as communion.

PUJA—Hindu worship consisting of mantras; the waving of incense and arati lamps; and the offering of flowers and fruits to a deity, group of deities, or holy persons.

R

RADHE—the wife of Lord Krishna, a manifestation of the Goddess Lakshmi.

RAMA—an incarnation of Lord Vishnu, a virtuous king.

RAMANANDA—the highest bliss of God.

RAVANA—the ten-headed king of the demons who stole Sita and took her to Sri Lanka in the Ramayana.

❖

RUDRAKSHA—a tree that produces a seed highly regarded by Lord Shiva, known as the tears of Lord Shiva. The tree also produces a bright blue fruit.

S

SADHAK—a spiritual aspirant doing sadhana.

SADHANA—your spiritual life program of yoga, mediation, and selfless service; this is what advances you.

SADHU—a holy man.

SAHIB—a respective title; a landowner; Sir.

SAMADHI—enlightened state of mental peace.

SANYASA—renunciation stage of life; holy wanderer.

SARASWATI—goddess of wisdom, music, and art.

SATSANG—community of spiritual persons.

SATTVAS—the pure state of balance.

SEVA—selfless service; karma yoga; work.

SHAKTI—spiritual energy, often identified with the Kundalini; a female consort of a male deity.

SHAKTIPA—enlightenment transferred from the Guru to his disciple in a flash of insight.

SHIVA CHALISA—hymns praising Lord Shiva.

SHIVA—Maheshwara, the great God of creation and destruction and recreation. Shiva means purity.

SHUDDRA—the lowest Indian caste, vaisya: common laborers, peasants, street sweepers, servants.

SIDDHIS—occult powers, miraculous powers and abilities.

SITA—the wife of Lord Rama, a manifestation on earth of the goddess Lakshmi.

SIVANANADA—a great Hindu swami with a large ashram in Rishikesh. The guru of Swami Satchidananda and Swami Shankarananda Giri.

SWAJAYA—the search for the Self through personal inquiry, asking "who am I;" deep introspection.

T

TANTRA—all aspects of your life made holy, even sex; often refers to the Kama Sutra; using the senses to merge with God.

TAPASYA—austerities, purification through heat, pain, and hardship, as a way of burning the ego.

TIFFIN—a snack taken in South India at four p.m., usually consisting of masala dosa, idli, and sambar.

TRISULA—Shiva's trident, or three-pronged pitch fork, a symbol of Sanyasa or Naga Babas, followers of Shiva.

U

UPAYA—method.

UDAS—a devotee of Anandamayi MA.

USHNISHA—Buddha's topknot of hair; hair pulled into a bun on the crown. MA wore this hair style.

V

VAIRAGHYA—aloof, dispassionate, no worldly desires.

VARNAKUM—"hello" in Tamil; the greeting of India.

VISHNU—the preserver of the Hindu trinity; the source of Rama, Krishna, Buddha, Christ, and MA.

VYASANA—a throne/seat of a guru or swami.

Y

YAGNA—a fire ceremony for an important occasion, usually based on ancient Vedic precepts. There is chanting and placing of objects in the fire, such as incense.

YOGA—from Yuj, to tie or connect yourself to something. Connecting yourself to life and to God, your body, truth, and enlightenment.

❖

the beginning of wisdom

Lord Krishna

❖

The end of all Knowledge

Is the beginning of Wisdom…"

—Sri Swami Nirmalanda of South India, a beloved Swami who lived in the forests, much like St. Francis, with the deer and birds, and in a high state of Enlightenment.

"We need to go beyond all thoughts and find Enlightenment…."

"The end of all Knowledge.

Is the beginning of Wisdom…"

Swami Ramananda

Dr. Swami Ramananda has a worldwide following of many thousands of people, with ashrams in Pondicherry, India; Los Angeles; and Palm Springs, California. He was initiated by Sri Anandamayi MA, and by Swami Shankarananda Giri, the head acharya of the Adi Parashakti Shiva Peetham in India, as his dharma successor. He has been devoted to Anandamayi MA since he was a teenager, and has traveled extensively in India over a seven-year period. Swamiji received his Bachelor's Degree Magna Cum Laude from California State University, San Jose, in Indian Philosophy and Yoga, with a minor in Indian Art, History, and Culture. He completed his Master's Degree at both the University of Madras and the University of California, Berkeley, in the Tamil religion of South India, with a focus on Goddess worship. He completed his Ph.D. in Indian Philosophy and Yoga from Shefferton University, London in 2002.

Swamiji is the President and Founder of the New Life Yoga Center International and the Jai Ma Foundation. He teaches yoga, and lectures extensively throughout the world. He has traveled recently to teach yoga in Greece, Egypt, India, Brazil, France, and England. Recently, he was a featured speaker at the Southwest Yoga Conference in Palm Springs, and has made many television appearances throughout the world, teaching yoga and sharing the life of Anandamayi MA.

Swamiji is a constantly joyous and blissful soul, and he only cares about bringing happiness and peace to this world. Other books by Swamiji include, *The Heart's Secret Door; Infinity*; and *Cry of the Eagle, Call of the Wolf*. Swamiji can be contacted at: P.O. Box 2931, Rancho Mirage, CA 92270, and via the web at http://www.swamiji.us, http://www.ILoveYoga.org, and BlissSwami@aol.com.

Swami: Infinity

Oh Swami, dear Swami,
I awaken at your feet
Watching Brother Sun, Sister Moon:
Even in your light sleep you chant, pray & sing

Oh Swami, dear Swami,
You bring us everything
Now my weary life resonates
Like a turquoise necklace and ring

Dear Swami, Swami,
Your songs lift my heart
It was heavy, troubled, and now I have wings
I soar with Mother and with Her, I sing

Dear Swami, oh Swami,
I can start to love and play, to chant songs
And dance each precious gem of day
Swami, Precious Swami,

Dearest Swami, Swamiji,
Your eyes are the stars
Your dance is a moonbeam
Your laughter is deep, an emerald stream

Oh Swami, dear Swami
Your eyes fill us with joy
You are streaks of pure sunshine
Holding us, your family, in your arms

Oh Swami, our Swami
We love you so very much
Your love is in each of our footsteps
Your love is a dance, a continuous poem

Oh Swami, beloved Swami,
You bring saints to our doors
You hug our sad hearts
We are flat on the floor

Swami, dear Swami
You bring us family and friends
We all sing and dance together
With you, the sweet movie never ends

Swami, Swami, Swami
You give us so much
You give us a new heart
With jeweled smiles, ornament hugs

Swami
Swami
Swami
We thank you
We love you
We are yours

Swami, Swami, Swami
You are the center of our world

—Prem Das

photo courtesy of Swami Ramananda

By chanting the Gayatri mantra, by performing fire sacrifice, and by doing japa, meditation and similar practices, one is cleansed and purified from the dross and karma accumulated during countless former births and in the present. Thereby is aided the unveiled revelation of that blazing, glorious Reality, which, like a readiant light, shines deep within oneselfm and which is the goal.

—Sri Sri Anandamayi MA, from Matri Vani

❖

BLISS NOW

166

Praise for *Bliss Now*

"Several years ago, as I was leading kirtans in the Los Angeles area, I noticed a man with a shaved head and orange robes sitting and swaying in the crowd, a huge smile on his face. When he came up to me afterward to say 'hi,' and 'thank you,' I was struck with the radiant heart energy that seemed to surround him. Gradually, we began to know each other better, and now I'm honored to call Swami Ramanada my friend. His life story is inspiring, as is his personal energy, and he shares both with no pretense, much joy, and abundant love. I cherish this book, as I cherish my friendship with Swamiji."

—Jai Uttal, Musician
http://www.jaiuttal.com

"Swami Ramananda's life has been blessed with darshan: the vision of the divine. Now Swami has put in book form his inspiration, his hope, and his encouragement for all of us to share his vision of divine light. His Mother was the Bliss-permeated One, and now he brings that bliss to each of us with clarity, poignancy, and infectious joy."

—David Life, Co-director of Jivamukti Yoga Center NYC
and Co-author of *Jivamukti Yoga: Practices for Liberating Body and Soul*

"*Bliss Now* is radiantly glowing with all of Ananadamayi Ma's lila. I am a teenager, and have worked with Swami Ramananda on many projects. He has not only become a friend, but the most life-altering teacher I have met. *Bliss Now* is glowing, it is ageless, and I have found such peace just from reading this book. This book is pure Anandamayi Ma. I have told everyone I know about Swamiji and his profound message. Swami's message is Bliss, love and light. Everyone who reads this book will undoubtedly experience the tranquility and laughter of Mother's amazing light."

—Tara Devi, 9th grade student,
Palm Desert High School, CA

"I feel so fortunate to know Swami Ramananda, or Swamiji, as he is affectionately called. He is the dancing, singing, joking, hugging, and light-filled teacher that I have been waiting to meet all of my life. Swamiji is a rare find, because he is a scholar who the shares beauty of the Hindu path without being heavy or preachy. His classes, whether they be dance yoga or Hindu 101, are deeply transformational. Swamiji's smiles and hugs are so full of Shakti that you find yourself glowing just by being in his presence. You will delight in his recounting of his experiences with Anandamayi Ma, because Mother's Light flows through Swamiji." If, like me, you loved *Be Here Now* by Ram Dass, and *It's Here Now, Are You?* by Bhagavan Dass, you'll know that *Bliss Now* is the trilogy that we've all been waiting for!"

—Deborah Meints, LMFT, Village Counseling Center, Palm Desert, CA

"Dr. Swami Ramananda's book is very impressive. His descriptions of India and travels with his guru, Sri Anandamayi Ma, are so rich and poetic. One feels transported to that ancient wonderful world of spiritual India in the 1960's and 1970's, when so many great teachers were living there. The final portion of *Bliss Now* is a 'how to' book to find spiritual happiness and balance in life. I would highly recommend this book to my patients as one of the finest books on New Age spirituality I have read. Furthermore, I feel that once you have read this book, you will never be the same. It's transformational."

—Dr. Betty Bandlow, M.D. Psychiatrist, St. Luke's Hospital, San Francisco

"Swami Ramananda is one of the most vital, inspirational teachers I have ever come across. He shares complex concepts in simple, easily-digestible words, combining them with his unique form of pure love and enthusiasm. Students of all ages benefit from his teachings; they are spiritual and psychological resources of the highest quality...."

—Ellen (Radha) Katz Brosamle, MS, LMFT, psychotherapist and producer/author, educational video: *When Helping Hurts, A Guide for the Enabler*